FROM THERE TO HERE

(WITH AN AWFUL LOT) IN BETWEEN

A MEMOIR

PAT BACKLEY

Pat Backley
www.patbackley.com

Paperback: ISBN: 978-0473-55974-8
Kindle: ISBN: 978-0-473-55976-2
Epub: ISBN: 978-0473-55975-5

Edited by: Colleen Ward.
Cover design by: 100 COVERS.
Formatted by: Formattedbooks.com

CONTENTS

ACKNOWLEDGEMENTS

I would like to thank all the wonderful people who have touched my life. There have been so many, some have played a huge part, others less so, but your influence has shaped me and made me the person I am today.

My greatest thanks must go to my parents, you gave me such a great start in life and I hope I have made you proud. I miss you both very much.

Without my beloved daughter Lucy, my life would have been far less meaningful. She is, without a doubt, the love of my life.

INTRODUCTION

mmigrant. Female, aged 69.

Me.

How did I get here?

It began in such an ordinary way. So far away. Halfway across the world.

I come from a long line of Londoners.

My ancestors were all working-class; dockers, hackney cab drivers, tailors, housemaids, tie cutters, match girls, cabinet makers, and factory workers.

People.

That's the key.

People. *That's* how my life is mapped out. *That's* how I got here.

I now realise that a memoir written by someone at 20 years old, 30 years old, or even 40 years old, is just an introduction. Honestly, even your 60s is really too soon. If you are lucky, there is still so much more to come.

But I digress.

It began in such an ordinary way.

Six pounds of scrawny white flesh. The firstborn of four to ordinary people living ordinary lives. Ordinary lives born of necessity, not by choice.

Since then my life has changed many times, always because of people.

Just in case you are interested, I will continue.

BACK TO THE BEGINNING

"Dear Aunt Rose,

Thought I would drop you a few lines to let you know that Miss Patricia Ann East has finally arrived. She was born in St Heliers Hospital at 9.25 on Easter Sunday morning and weighed six pounds, 8 ounces. No idea who she looks like, she has quite a lot of dark hair, but she's certainly a sleepyhead like George.

With lots of love,
Doris"

So began my public introduction to this world. My Great Aunt Rose, being something of a dabbler in astrology, promptly sat down and did my birth reading horoscope.

Despite the allusion to my father's penchant for sleep, this letter, written by my mother to her aunt, barely conceals the pride and joy she felt at having successfully produced her firstborn child.

You may be thinking this is not such an amazing feat, but for Mum, it was something of a miracle. She had grown up as a poor child in the slums of London, and had suffered from rickets and other serious health issues. She had been led to believe that she would never be able to bear children. Having grown up with this knowledge, she had made it quite plain to my father on the day he proposed that she longed for a family. They had discussed adoption, but did not think they would have biological children.

Needless to say, two years after their marriage I defied the medical world and was followed in succeeding years by two baby sisters and one baby brother!

When I was born in 1951, England was still recovering from the devastating effects of World War 2.

Although technically we had won the war, it was at a great cost. Housing was in extremely short supply, as were food and clothing. Food rationing was still in existence and by all accounts, my only contribution to these shortages was to devour my parents' meat and cheese rations as well as my own.

Due to the lack of suitable housing, my parents were forced to live with my paternal grandparents at their council house in Rosehill in Surrey.

Rosehill is a sprawling estate, designed in the early 1930s to rehouse families from London. Today it appears to be just a stone's throw from Central London, but at the time my grandparents moved there as a young couple with a small son it must have seemed a million light-years away from the crowded, noisy, dirty streets and tenements of Southwark.

The estate was designed with solid brick houses, each with a small garden. There was plenty of green open space for children to play, and of course very few cars. Everyone on the estate was a council tenant, almost all Cockneys, so there was great camaraderie. It must have been difficult for all those people to adjust at first to a new life in brand new houses away from their close-knit family groups. Surrounded by fields, instead of buildings of the city.

My grandfather was a docker, so he had to travel up to the city of London from the estate every day. Fortunately the London Underground (the Tube) station at Morden was just a ten-minute bus ride away, but it still meant leaving home at five in the morning.

My parents spent the first six years of their marriage in the house in Rosehill, and it was to be my home until I reached the age of three and a half (that's when I became the proud owner of a new baby sister).

Mum, Dad, and I lived in the tiny bedroom that had been my father's before his marriage, and I understand from Mum that we also shared the small space with his pushbike. That was something of a bone of contention between my parents, I think.

Apparently I was quite a good child, but did have the appalling habit of waking extremely early (usually about 5.30am), jumping onto my parents' bed (which, of course, in such a small room, was easily reached from my cot), and singing nursery rhymes to them until they awakened.

I can remember lots of very long walks with Mum - walking was cheap and got her away from the claustrophobic atmosphere of the shared home. Sometimes we would go to the local park and like most small children, I loved the freedom of the wide open spaces.

There are few photos taken from that time, all the adults look a bit tense whilst I, blissfully unaware of any problems, happily indulge in private games with my new teddy bear. In the photos, Teddy is seen as a rather handsome chap with beautiful, thick, yellow fur. He is a prime example of bear manhood. But oh, how the years have mistreated him. I still love and cherish that bear, but today he is merely a shadow of his former glorious self. There is hardly any fur remaining to keep him warm, his poor ears are remarkably battered (due, I suspect, to my constant chewing on them as a child), and his once-muscular legs have now completely caved in at the thighs. Much of his stuffing has long since gone and - the final indignity - he is no longer capable of raising a squeak, let alone the splendid grunt he once could.

When he was about 40 years old and looking particularly down in the dumps, I gave him a complete facelift. He got new leather patches on his poor worn elbows and feet, freshly embroidered eyes, and a bright red ribbon to wear around his old wrinkled neck. But if we are being frank, Teddy and I both knew the truth. He had enjoyed a wildly misspent youth and all the beauty treatments in the world would never restore him to his former glory.

I was three years old when we moved to Longmere Gardens, Tadworth, in leafy Surrey, just a few miles from Epsom Downs Racecourse, home of the Derby.

We lived in a brand new house on a newly-built council estate, surrounded by fields, farm, and heathland. The farm was particularly exciting, as it meant we could go and visit the new-born lambs in springtime and talk to the chickens and horses every time we passed them on our way to Burgh Heath.

At that time in the early 1950s, Burgh Heath, which was situated about six miles south of Sutton on the main London to Brighton road, was a sleepy little village.

It had a few interesting little shops, including a pet shop on the edge of the village green. Here, we were allowed to choose our own goldfish using a little net to remove them from the big glass tank and dropping them carefully into a plastic bag to take home. It was such an innocent pleasure, but I remember being hugely thrilled every time, after a suitable period of mourning, I was allowed to go and choose another fish as a "replacement pet."

There was a fascinating draper's shop with old-fashioned wooden cabinets full of brightly coloured buttons, ribbons, and lace. The shop was owned by two charming ladies whom I thought were pretty ancient, but they were probably only in their early fifties at the time.

There was a butcher's shop with men in striped aprons and sawdust on the floor. Apparently Mum hated going in there, as she was something of a prude and they took great delight in teasing the shy young housewife by making risqué comments about "nice legs or breasts" (of lamb, I presume). This was long before the days of political correctness, and I don't think it helped that Dad found it funny when she later recounted the tales.

Then there was Detes Stores, a rather musty general provisions shop, run by two elderly sisters who kept geese in their backyard. The geese were obviously not too fond of customers, as they would hiss and try to chase you away if you approached from the rear and got too close.

The little village also housed a couple of little antique bric-a-brac shops in the tiny cottages that surrounded the pond.

The village boasted two swimming pools, one at the Sugar Bowl and the other at the Galleon Country Club, two pubs, a racehorse training stable, and a Shell garage, where my Dad worked occasionally on the weekends.

Sadly, it has all quite changed with the time.

The cottages surrounding the pond have almost all been demolished and replaced with modern townhouses. Most of the shops, both pubs, and the racing stables have all gone for redevelopment. The Sugar Bowl is now a Premier Inn and the Galleon Country Club and small Shell garage have made way for a huge and more modern petrol station.

When I was young, I had no idea that living on a council estate meant that some people viewed us as second-class citizens.

That awful realisation was to hit me later, when I encountered snobbery for the first time.

This was simply my home, where I belonged. Where Mum, Dad, and my baby sister, Carol, were. Where I felt safe and loved.

The move to Tadworth was not easy for either of my parents, despite my comfort with it.

Mum was not excited by her brand new home, even though the little brick house was a sturdy, well-built, and modern design. It was an instantly recognisable bog-standard council house of the era.

The kitchen and hallway were at the front of the house, with small high windows, designed for privacy. This meant that unless you sat on the staircase and peered through the narrow window, it was impossible to see what was going on in the street outside.

She longed to live in one of the houses opposite. They were much the same design as ours, but with big picture windows in the lounge area and the bedrooms, all facing the street. For the entire time she lived there, almost 13 years, she felt a sense of acute disappointment that we had been given an inferior property.

Dad, on the other hand, had problems of his own.

He had a good job as an electronics engineer, but now that he lived in the country, he had to spend a lot more time on public transport, travelling to and from work.

Faced with not *quite* enough money to make ends meet, an unhappy wife, a happy but probably rather demanding small daughter (me), and a new baby, it all became a bit too much.

As the only surviving and much-loved son of his parents, who had, apart from spending the war years in South Africa with the RAF, always lived at home and was cosseted by his adoring mother, it must have come as a shock for him to suddenly have so much responsibility.

Sadly, he had a nervous breakdown and was hospitalised for almost six months, during which time he was given electric shock therapy.

I had no knowledge of this at the time, other than being aware that my Dad was "ill" and knowing I missed him. Until then we had been good companions, often going for walks together, hand in hand, the both of us pigeon-toed. I wrote to him regularly and sent little drawings, but I was not allowed to visit while he was away.

I can remember sitting on the top deck of the bus, pointing to the old hospital on the hill at Belmont and announcing in a loud voice that "My dad had been in there for ages." Mum was understandably mortified, as back in the 1950s, mental illness was far more taboo than it is today. It must have been extremely hard for her, coping while he was away with two small children and very little income in a new environment and no family support.

Dad came home eventually, with a rather nice wooden coffee table which he had made during therapy classes. Normal life resumed, or, so we thought. I was thrilled to have him back, but his illness had changed our family dynamic forever.

Eventually, a little brother came along.

Our house only had two bedrooms, so I found myself sharing a room with both of my siblings. This was not a problem for me, as it meant that if I was cold, or having a bad dream and didn't want to risk crossing the landing to Mum and Dad's room, in case the crocodiles came to get me, I could just snuggle in beside my sister Carol (much to her disgust, as apparently I fidgeted all night)

As a child, I enjoyed being at home all day. In the 1950s, very few married women worked, so Mum was always there for us and the idea of nursery school was never even considered.

I remember long, sunny days, playing with my dolls in the garden, making tents with sheets draped across the washing line, playing hide-and-seek in the bushes and just generally having fun. I was very fond of chatting to the neighbours over the garden fence, Mrs. Cousins on one side and Mrs. Webbon on the other. Sometimes I think I was a little too chatty for Mum's taste; she would often call me inside and explain that not everything should be discussed with the neighbours.

Soon enough, it all changed. I was five years old, and I had to go to school.

The recollections of my very early school days are somewhat hazy, and I tend now to only remember isolated incidents. Time, as they say, is certainly a great healer and although I had some very unhappy moments at school, the times I remember most vividly now are the funny and happy ones.

I began my education at the tiny village church school at Burgh Heath.

Sadly, this was closed down and demolished many years ago, but at the time it was a lovely little school next to the pond with a large, shady tree in the playground.

There were only two classes, one for infants and the other for juniors. I don't remember learning much of any academic value in that first year, but I do recall long nature walks and P.E. lessons on the Heath and sitting cross-legged under the big tree in the afternoons whilst our teacher read stories to us.

Every lunchtime we marched, crocodile style, across the main Brighton Road to eat our school dinners in the village hall.

I vividly remember the ever-pervading smell of carbolic soap in the school toilets and nowadays, I only have to catch a slight whiff of carbolic and I am instantly transported back through the years to that tiny school.

The outstanding incident of those first few months at school was surely a pointer of things to come.

Due to my incessant chatter, our poor teacher finally lost her patience and dispatched me to the corner of the classroom to drink my regulation daily third of a pint of milk, provided by the government, in solitude.

The milk was icy cold despite my attempts to warm it up over the radiator, and I felt utterly miserable and dejected as I stood there, my back to the rest of the class, tears of self-pity streaming down my little face.

It turns out that I did not learn at all from that sad incident, as over the years since, many people have remarked on my ability to out-chatter anyone else.

The next school I attended was to be my favourite: Shawley County Primary School, Epsom Downs. It still exists today, although whether its current pupils love it as much as I did, I cannot guess.

One reason for the popularity was undoubtedly the lovely head-master – Mr. Baker. He was a very kind man, always approachable, and because of this, he earned great respect and loyalty from both pupils and parents.

His right hand and deputy was the rather formidable Mrs. Briddell, and together they appeared to be an excellent team for the care and handling of several hundred children. In this happy atmo-sphere, I spent my formative years between the ages of six and eleven.

When I was just six years old, I fulfilled a long-held ambition. I had, for a very long time, wanted to be sick during school assembly. This desire was due to several observations I had made on these occasions in the past. Firstly, the sheer drama of it all appealed very much to me. The sudden notoriety of causing a scene during the hymns and having the entire school's eyes fixed firmly on me? I loved the thought. Secondly, there was the semi-permanent reminder it would leave of the event for everyone to see, for after clearing up the mess, the caretaker would sprinkle sawdust on the wooden floor and it would remain there for the rest of the day. Lastly, but certainly not least, the main objective of the whole affair – it would give me the remainder of the day off school, after having been driven home in the headmaster's car.

I made my plans and got ready for the execution of this event. When the big day dawned, I, perhaps foolishly, decided to confide in Marilyn, one of my new-found friends. Having listened with great respect to my plan, she agreed wholeheartedly that it was a wonderful idea. However, she had one suggestion. Could I possibly manage to be sick all over her, so that she would also be allowed to leave school? This seemed like a very reasonable request, and I happily agreed to do my best.

As we marched into the assembly, I was mentally preparing for the ordeal to come, for I was under no illusion as to the magnitude of the unpleasant task I had set myself.

Into the second hymn I had begun to feel sick for real, and there was no difficulty in producing the goods. In the final moment I remembered my promise to Marilyn and did not falter. The deed was done amidst the fully anticipated shocked reaction of my classmates, who were not aware that it was self-induced.

Marilyn and I were borne off to the school nurse and duly mopped up. Then, to my great joy, Mr. Baker appeared like an administering angel with the offer to drive us home.

I don't think I shall ever forget the sight that greeted us as we turned the corner onto my road. Mum was cleaning the top landing window, perching precariously on the ledge, and was so surprised to see me arriving home five hours too early *and* in the headmaster's car, she nearly fell out of the window.

I was gently deposited on the living room sofa by that kind man, who told Mum that I had been most unwell and that it would probably be advisable to keep me at home for a day or two. I am not ashamed to admit that I did feel more than a twinge of guilt at so utterly deceiving these two delightful people.

The true blessing that came out of the whole sorry farce was that from that day on, Marilyn became my very close friend and remained so throughout our primary school days. I often wonder if many little girls go to such lengths to attract friendships, though I think ours was special in that way.

The next event I remember was extremely unfortunate, and almost certainly *lost* me a friend rather than gained me one.

By the occurrence of this next ordeal, I was seven or eight years old and feeling very grown up. One wet playtime, I offered to style a few of my classmates' hair. Of course, I had absolutely no formal hairdressing experience, just plain optimism and the assurance that in no time at all, I could turn my friends into budding beauties.

I began with great confidence and had no major mishaps, until I decided to turn my artistic talents to the head of a little girl with long, blonde locks. I convinced her that with a twirl or two of my magic comb - the only piece of hairdressing equipment I was in possession of at the time - she would be the proud owner of a beautiful head of curls that would be the envy of the entire school.

I confidently wound her beautiful straight hair round and round my comb until it resembled a fat sausage, all the while my admiring audience was gasping at my audacity. However, all of a sudden, with a sickening feeling growing in the pit of my stomach, I realised that something had gone terribly wrong. As hard as I tried, I couldn't get the damned comb out of that rolled up sausage of locks. Smiling brightly, I informed my audience and now-panicking client that this was *supposed* to be happening, and was indeed the only way of ensuring a truly tight curl.

I had absolutely no idea what I was doing and in my desperation I began tugging for all I was worth. Great lumps of hair began ripping out of my poor victim's head and she, now utterly distraught, changed her muffled sobs to great moans and cries. The more I tugged, the more she screamed.

By the time a teacher arrived on the scene, I think we were all in varying forms of distress; it was obviously not a pretty sight. Within minutes, the poor woman had taken control of the situation and did her best to comfort both victim and torturer alike. A fair amount of the offending hair had to be cut away to get the comb out and at the end of it, the poor, innocent creature certainly did not have the super Vidal Sassoon look I had rashly promised her. Heavens only knows what havoc I could have wreaked had I possessed a pair of scissors and a set of heated rollers.

Not all my early school days were marred by such self-imposed tragedies, but I did seem to have more than my fair share of traumas. Looking back at old school reports, it was often said that I was rather musical with a good sense of rhythm, so it is lost on me why I always got the boring old triangle to play in the school orchestra instead of something exotic like the drums or the tambourine. How I longed to be one of the stars of the class instead of the little retiring creature I believed myself to be, and how far I dared myself to go to get there.

This feeling was to remain with me for many years - always feeling slightly inferior to my peers. It is only now, as I have gotten much older, that I have come to regard myself as someone who is good enough, with her own "thing" to contribute to the world to help make it a nicer, happier place to be. What a lot of very hard lessons we all have to learn along the way.

Despite these feelings of inferiority, I was always a sociable little girl, never happier than when part of a group and having fun. I always had a great desire to be "in with the in crowd!" To this end of being socially acceptable, I made some gestures which went against the grain of my beliefs and morals, but were nevertheless, at the time, considered to be acceptable losses in my desperate desire to belong.

Several girls I admired at primary school came from much wealthier homes than I, and it became their custom, each lunch-time, to state loudly just how disgusting they found the food offered for our consumption. Actually, the school dinners were extremely good, very varied and nourishing, with such delights as strawberry shortcake and roast beef. As I had never been a faddy eater anyway, I was more than content with my lunchtime lot.

After a while though, I began to feel that perhaps it was childish to be so easy to please. With a desperate need to belong to what I believed was that "elitist group," I too began to grumble at lunchtime. The only thing I truly hated was butter beans, so that was a good place to start. However, having realised that one complaint wasn't going to be enough to ingratiate myself, I set out to develop more.

In the end, my true nature won. I was only able to adopt a stand on the dreaded butter beans and cheese pie - neither of which was served often. Having convinced the school cooks by this time that I would truly die of food poisoning if they forced me to eat these wretched items, I felt I had gained ascendancy to the required plane and was able to boast with equanimity that I too, was discerning enough to despise school dinners.

After the aforementioned dinners, we were, if the weather permitted, sent out onto the school playing fields. Once freed from the shackles of supervision we became a little crazy, and those wide open spaces allowed us to indulge in all sorts of imaginative play.

One particular afternoon it was very hot, and having exhausted all energetic games, it was decided that we should do something exciting but reasonably stationary. To this end, we all unbuckled our shoes and took turns kicking them off our feet. The idea was that the person who managed to kick the highest would be pronounced the winner. There were quite a few of us involved, both boys and girls, and I think we were probably aged about nine or ten.

I do remember, most vividly, that when it came to be my turn, I was extremely anxious to do well as I was sure this was the best way to gain popularity. I reasoned that if determination was enough, my kicking skills would easily match those of my friends. Unfortunately, I was, as usual, a little too optimistic and kicked off with rather too much vigour. The first of my new red leather Clarks summer sandals landed disappointingly, without reaching a great height. However, in the horror of all horrors, the other sandal, having been kicked with gay abandon, flew over the fence into the neighbouring private garden. Just at that moment, the bell rang announcing the end of our lunch break.

One of the boys gallantly dangled me, headfirst, over the fence in an attempt to retrieve the offending article, but with no success. By now, all the other children had filed back into school and one of the teachers came over to see why we had not obeyed the bell. Without discussion, we knew that kicking our shoes off would not be considered a suitable pastime, so nothing was mentioned and we meekly marched back, under the teacher's watchful eye, to begin our afternoon lessons. Miraculously, nobody seemed to notice my peculiar gait, due to one shoe off and one shoe on, but I sat there all afternoon in a state of terror, awaiting the dreaded summons from the headmaster.

Fortunately, the owner of the garden must have been away that afternoon, for no irate adult turned up bearing a red sandal and demanding the incarceration of its owner. After school had finished for the day, one of the boys very kindly jumped over the fence and retrieved my lost shoe, which I had been utterly convinced I was destined never to see again. I think the whole incident gave us a bit of a fright though, for we never played such a silly game again, at least, not quite so close to the edge of the field.

For a while after that, my need to belong was not strong enough to overcome the overriding fear of punishment for crimes committed, so I settled into a more relaxed existence and acquired several close and rewarding friendships. Most of these were recorded for posterity in my "Princess Friendship Book" and make for fascinating reading (mainly to discover what the interests were of nine and ten year old girls back in 1960).

I expect that today, most of these girls grew to be wives, mothers, and even grandmothers, living ordinary, happy lives. But oh, what exotic dreams we had. To own a tight skirt and meet Tommy Steele and Tony Curtis was our ideal. Most of us probably achieved the tight skirt eventually, but I'm not sure if any of us ever met Tony Curtis.

For a while, we became rather romantically inclined and formed our very own fan club. The hero of the hour was William Russell from *The Adventures of Sir Lancelot*, and we each had to keep a special "club" picture of him. I still have mine somewhere and think they came from packets of bubble gum!

We had secret codes and became quite devoted, even going so far as to write to him, although we unwittingly ruined our chances of a personal reply from the great man himself by forgetting to include a stamped and addressed envelope. Undeterred, we continued to admire him from afar and for a while, during each lunch break, the school playing field would become our stage as we enacted scenes from the TV show. As you would expect, there was great rivalry for the star roles of Sir Lancelot, Queen Guinevere, and King Arthur, but there were plenty of calls for extras and lots of us just waltzed around with flimsy bits of fabric swathed around our heads, pretending to be ladies of the court. Needless to say it was great fun, and for those of us with artistic ambitions, it merely fueled our fires. As far as I can remember, the passion for this particular hero was fairly short-lived, but my enthusiasm for fame and notoriety on stage was not - as you have already witnessed!

I took to expanding my theatrical experiences at home, and, having a younger brother and sister, found no shortage of willing co-stars. Most of our productions were short and passed unnoticed by all but ourselves, but there were one or two notable exceptions. With delusions of grandeur even at such a tender age, I decided to form my own theatrical company. This illustrious band was henceforth known as "The Special Three," and consisted of myself, brother, Michael, and sister, Carol. Productions were sometimes spiced up a little by the addition of my charming and sophisticated friend and neighbour, Miss Lorraine Parker, but as she was only an occasional (albeit very welcome) guest artist, I remained, for all intents and purposes, the "boss."

Most of these performances faded very quickly into artistic oblivion, but a few remain firmly etched in my mind.

One was a summer concert that we performed solely for the benefit of our loving parents. After some intense discussion, we decided to hold this in Lorraine's garden, due to the fact that her garden shed lent itself very well to be used as a star's dressing room. It was unquestionably a better space than Dad's shed, as it would certainly have been most uncomfortable, if not impossible, to relax between costume changes whilst perched precariously on the piles of old television sets and rather rusty boxes of old tools!

The next administrative decision to be taken was probably one of the most important to ensure a successful production: What do we serve as refreshments in the interval to our illustrious guests? As usual, the final menu decided upon was orange squash and biscuits, and to be fair to our long-standing parents, not only did they valiantly sit through our lengthy and not wildly exciting summer variety shows (consisting mainly of off-key singing, a little ballet and tap dancing, and a few wonderfully presented sketches), but they also dutifully and quite uncomplainingly paid up the requested pennies we charged for their admission, programmes, and refreshments. The refreshments came from their own kitchens and were re-charged to them at an exorbitant price!

The fact that we were fortunate enough to have loving and kind parents who in no way decried our efforts only spurred us on to greater achievements.

My enthusiasm for a theatrical career was further enhanced by a wonderful trip, with my friend Gillian and her father, to see a pantomime at the London Palladium. I was invited to go at the last moment because Gillian's mother was unwell. I was tremendously excited as it meant travelling all the way to London by train, which was a rare treat for me. I can still vividly remember the thrill of watching Harry Secombe, Roy Castle, and others perform. I forget what the show was called now, but it certainly included all the necessary additives, like a baddie, a beautiful fairy, and lots of noisy audience participation. Afterwards, feeling thoroughly drunk with excitement, we had to wait at Waterloo Station for the next train home and as there was some delay, Gillian's dad bought mugs of tomato soup to keep us warm. This soup has remained a wonderful, tangible memory and even now, I still optimistically partake of the occasional paper cup of tomato soup, courtesy of British Rail. Of course, it never, ever tastes nearly as good as that first one.

My artistic interest was by no means limited to the theatre, however, as I also planned to become a best-selling author and started on that path by creating and editing a magazine. This magazine was carefully planned to contain just the right amount of diversity to attract my audience *and* included a page with competitions - the first prize being a desirable propelling pencil. There were assorted editorials on music, dancing, pets, clothes, and hairdressing, as well as the expected fiction pages. While I was thrilled for my new venture, in the end, it proved to be a task of such magnitude that this editor - at the tender age of nine or ten - only managed to produce one limited edition of what was meant to be a weekly production.

Undaunted by letting go of that plan, I returned to an old love… ballet dancing.

One of my earliest ambitions was to become a ballerina, and I had visions of floating around the stage at Sadler's Wells. Sadly, my parents couldn't afford to send me to ballet lessons, but, undeterred, I set about teaching myself.

From the church jumble sale, I acquired a book that explained the basic steps of ballet. From then on, it was smooth sailing. Stiffnet petticoats were very fashionable at that time, and my sister and I each owned a pale blue one which had been passed down from some affluent friends. These petticoats, when worn over our vests and knickers, doubled up beautifully as tutus.

While my ballet craze was at its height, my sister and I gave regular performances to captive audiences. In reality, these usually consisted of just long-suffering enthusiasts like our parents.

Our repertoire was comprehensive, with a fair smattering of such classics as *The Tempest* and *Midsummer Night's Dream* performed to music. However, our real favourite was "Dance of the Sugar Plum Fairies."

This passion for the ballet was further fuelled by a trip with my friend Marilyn and her mother to see the ballet at Covent Garden, and later going to the Granada cinema in Sutton to watch a documentary on the Russian Bolshoi Ballet.

For many years I dreamt in vain of owning a proper tutu and pink satin ballet slippers, and I was wildly envious of any little girl lucky enough to do so.

My drawings of that time depicted dark-haired girls, resplendent in glorious technicoloured ballet attire; I have no doubt who they were meant to represent!

As a poor second to learning ballet from the greats, I came to love the country dancing lessons we had at school. For these I was well enough equipped, as all you needed was a little agility, a pair of plimsolls, and a pretty summer dress. Mum always made sure our dresses were lovely, even when it meant sitting up all night sewing before a special event. Somehow, she always managed to scrape together the money each year to make us a new one.

There are two particular dresses that I remember with great affection.

One was a beautiful fairy dress for the school Christmas play. Mum made it out of pink and white satin and net, and I was very proud when I unpacked it at school because it was so stiff that it stood up on the desk all by itself. The other one was made for a country dancing display at a neighbouring school; it was made of white cotton fabric and covered in tiny pink and red flowers. I felt so beautiful wearing it; it was as if I had magic dust in my plimsolls and I danced on air for the whole afternoon. I don't suppose for a minute that my improved dancing was obvious to anyone else, but in my mind, that afternoon, I was definitely world-class material.

I was only a tiny little girl at that time (and indeed was to remain smaller than average until I reached puberty at fifteen) but my dancing partner was even smaller. His name was John Sullivan and he was an extremely nice, gentle boy with freckles and glasses. Looking back, what sympathy I have for that poor young man. Once I got into the swing of things, I became, as usual, fired up with enthusiasm, and would whirl around wildly, whisking poor John off his feet and making him quite dizzy! Like the true gentleman he was, even at the tender age of nine or ten he never once complained. I often think that he must have grown up into a really nice man, well able to withstand the rigours of female excesses.

The farmland surrounding our house was sold when I was about nine years old. It was going to be redeveloped as a trend-setting comprehensive school and another new housing estate.

Although it was strictly forbidden, my friends and I often used to take a shortcut across the fields on our way home from school. Apart from the normal excitement induced by defying parental instructions, other incidents occurred which added fuel to my theory that defiance was sometimes the only way of experiencing life's finer things.

For example, on one very memorable occasion, I came face to face with an Indian carpet seller.

Complete with an exotic carpet bag and looking splendid in a bright turban, he was sitting by the side of the road as we climbed over the gate leading from the field. He had obviously been re-arranging the wares in his bag, for a beautiful Indian rug was open and spread across the ground. As he looked up and saw us, a wide smile spread across his very dark face, exposing pearly white teeth.

I was terrified, particularly when my friend Marjorie whispered that she had heard how men like him captured children and then brought them far, far away in carpet bags.

Now, I have never been lacking in imagination. You can only guess what my little mind made of that remark, particularly as the only other people I had ever come across with skins darker than my own were West Indians I had seen occasionally on the London Underground.

This chap seemed to be an altogether different proposition. For a start, he was a very exotic-looking creature and this alone seemed to me to be an indication that what Marjorie intimated was perhaps true. Of course, capturing two little girls was the very last thing on this poor man's mind; he was probably just brushing up his sales patter before knocking on the next door. But we ran home as if the devil himself was after us and for several weeks thereafter, we could not summon enough courage to take that way home!

This fear was remarkably short-lived of course, and it was not long before we were again confident enough to face anything. That was, until we met Dougie.

Dougie was a very large Teddy Boy with bright ginger hair and one earring. Back in the fifties in rural Tadworth, that was *quite* unusual.

We had seen him before, at a safe distance and in the protected company of our parents, but to meet him at 8.30 on a sunny morning when you were quite alone was altogether different. He was sitting, propped up beside the telephone box, and although he never did or said, anything remotely threatening, I was absolutely terrified and would go miles out of my way to avoid meeting him. He had acquired a fearsome reputation, mainly due I think to the earring and the fact that he had been expelled from several schools. He probably enjoyed terrorising little girls merely by looking mysterious.

For a very long time even after I was quite grown up, I would pass that phone box with a certain amount of trepidation, for over the years my fertile imagination had built Dougie up into someone quite alarming. I did see him again once, years later when I was sixteen, and was absolutely amazed to discover how small he really was and not at all scary. In fact, he even gave me a wolf-whistle, which did wonders for my morale as a self-conscious teenager and helped bury that particular bogeyman theory forever.

We had quite a long walk to school, short-cuts not-withstanding, and sometimes we would meet another girl on the way. I can't remember her name anymore, but I remember her ideas vividly. She was a year older than us and therefore considered herself to be something of an expert on current and world affairs, her particular speciality being wars and the end of the world. A little unusual for a ten-year-old, if I'm to be honest.

She was quite sure that there would very shortly be a third world war and was knowledgeable enough to inform me that all men over the age of eighteen and below the age of forty would automatically be called up for duty. She made sure to note that these men would all very probably be killed defending their country. As my dad was not yet forty, I was absolutely petrified to hear this. Not feeling able to confide in my parents - as I was quite sure they must be worried enough already about this impending war - I kept this dreadful information to myself and spent many a sleepless night worrying about how I would cope being a fatherless child.

This morbid young lady also enjoyed talking about her predictions for the end of the world. I was impressionable, but not quite gullible enough to swallow the idea that a ten-year-old girl could predict such an event. Unfortunately though, at that time in the late 1950s, there seemed to be plenty of other people willing to predict a similar end. Having half-believed her stories, I was horrified to hear on the radio that the world was going to end at 3.30 on a particular Thursday afternoon.

The dreaded day dawned, and it was all I could think about as I sat at my lessons. My poor, tortured little mind was worrying about how I could possibly run home in 15 minutes (school didn't end till 3.15) to be with my mum when the moment came. I couldn't quite understand why all the teachers were so relaxed and seemingly unconcerned about the end of the world, but finally reasoned that perhaps adults always behaved that way in times of crisis. After all, my own parents had not spent breakfast time weeping and wailing, either.

At last the bell rang, and I ran home as fast as my little legs would carry me. I remember that it was a very hot summer's day, and as I ran tears were pouring down my face, for I was so frightened that the bomb would go off before I saw my darling family ever again.

Of course, as with all such predictions, nothing happened. However, it was a very long time before I could face up to my unspoken fear of such a thing really coming true. Consequently, I learned to avoid that war-loving child like the plague!

At home, I was something of a ringleader.

Being the eldest, I felt it was my responsibility to teach my little sister and brother everything I knew.

This included such things as trampolining on our beds on Sunday mornings until we were exhausted. I then trained them to lie there, singing hymns at the top of their voices until Mum yelled at us to stop.

When we played "School," I was always the very bossy teacher in charge of "The Primrose School for Young Ladies and Gentlemen." Here, any small misdemeanours would be punished by a tap on the desk with my wooden ruler. If my siblings really annoyed me, I think I may occasionally have "accidently" rapped one of them over the knuckles, although generally I was never in favour of capital punishment.

One of our favourite games, which drove Mum crazy, was pulling faces while we were sitting at the table waiting for dinner to be served. If she caught us doing this she would get cross, and when occasionally we really overstepped the mark and misbehaved during a meal, she would threaten us with the stick in the sideboard. She never smacked any of us, although at times I am sure we deserved it. The mere threat of the stick was enough to keep us all in line. It was only years later when we were all grown up that we realised that the stick did not even exist! On a few occasions we must have driven her really crazy, because she told us that if we didn't start to behave, she was going to send us to live at a children's home. This was at a time when there were many such places, so I guess we thought the threat was quite real.

Sometimes, on dark and wintry Sunday evenings, Mum would turn on the radio for one of her favourite programmes, "Sing Something Simple." Within a few minutes we would all be waltzing around the room. She even used to persuade Dad to join in.

On our birthdays, we always woke to find a trail of cards leading from the front door to our little pile of presents. She would often have sat up half the night to make us a new dress or some clothes for our dolls.

For one birthday, I received the most beautiful little black doll and she became a great favourite. A couple of years later, our church held an appeal for toys for poor children in Africa, and I went home full of enthusiasm for the idea. My generosity was limited however, to things I no longer had any use for, which were decidedly on the tatty side. Mum gently explained that giving meant more if what you gave away was something that you actually valued.

With a heavy heart, I decided that my little black doll had to go, and so Mum knitted her some new pink clothes.

She looked so beautiful, sitting under the Christmas tree at church with all the other donated toys; it nearly broke my heart. But when the minister spoke of the boys and girls whose Christmas morning would be enriched by our generosity, I began to feel better, imagining the look of delight on a little African girl's face when she opened her present.

I was only young and it was a hard lesson to learn, but I am very glad I learned it, for I have found that giving is one of life's greatest joys.

We were of course, very lucky to have such a caring and kind mother and this more than made up for our lack of money and material possessions.

I was always aware that we were not as well-off financially as other families. Our pocket money was much less than my friends' and was often hard to come by. We looked forward to the man coming to empty the gas or electricity meter; it was always a red letter day because he left us a rebate of a big pile of shillings (probably worth about one pound each in today's money).

Looking back, I really don't know how Mum managed to feed and clothe us all on the little she had.

Washdays must have been a nightmare, for she insisted that we all wore a clean blouse or shirt every day and she didn't own a washing machine or tumble dryer. I can remember coming home from school on Mondays to find her toiling over the old copper boiler, the kitchen full of steam, only to then have to put it all through the old wringer by the back door before hanging it on the line to dry. Drying the clothes on wet days and in the winter must have been another nightmare, as we had no heating - just an open coal fire in the lounge.

Feeding us couldn't have been much fun either, but we certainly never starved. She made lots of nourishing stews with dumplings and often without meat, not from choice as vegetarians would, but from necessity, as there was never quite enough money to buy it. There were rice puddings with delicious, brown, crunchy tops, jam tarts, cheese straws, and apple pies. Occasionally, when we were allowed to indulge, there was bread and dripping.

Once Mum went back to work and spent her hard-earned wages on the household, there was little room for luxuries like plaice beautifully cooked in breadcrumbs or the occasional lamb chop. I can remember the meat man coming to the estate in his shiny van and the thrill of following Mum up the steps to the counter to see what she would choose this week; perhaps a pound of steak and kidney for one of her delicious pies or maybe just some mince and a few oxo cubes for a tasty stew.

She always tried to ensure there were enough pennies to give us our pocket money and would religiously hand over my 3d every

Friday. Dad however, from whom the other half came, was a little stingier; often we would be found on a Saturday morning grovelling at his feet before we could be off to the sweet shop. Once there, we would indulge in such delights as cough candies or rhubarb and custard boiled sweets, Black Jack and Fruit Salad chews, flying saucers, sherbet dips, pink shrimps, chocolate bananas, and sweet cigarettes. Mum never approved of the sweet cigarettes; she thought they would give us bad habits in the future and she would get cross if we wasted all our money on a Jamboree Bag. According to her, they were "a swizzle, just out to cheat kids of their money through good advertising."

My lifelong affinity for sweets and chocolate meant I had great difficulty in saving much money, although for a time I was quite determined to do so because I passionately wanted a bike.

I covered an old shoe box with scraps of leftover wallpaper, cut a hole in the top, and, in my very best writing, labelled it, "PAT'S BIKE FUND."

Sadly there were too many calls on my pennies, and after almost a year and only three shillings and two pence halfpenny saved, I decided to be a miser no longer. I had even saved one of the half-crowns my paternal granddad had given me, but it was still nowhere near enough. Needless to say, I didn't manage to own a bike until many, many years later.

Another, far more satisfactory way of gaining possessions was via the rag-and-bone man who called from time to time. In the old days he had a horse and cart, but in my day he drove a little van, suddenly appearing at the top of our road unannounced, save for the tinkling of his horn.

This was the signal for us children to stop playing and rush indoors to beg Mum to quickly unearth sufficient rags for us each to get a good present from him. The idea seemed to be that you gave him two and a half tons of rags, and in return he gave you a dying goldfish or a notepad and pen. At the time, we children thought it was an excellent exchange.

We used to have lovely family Christmases when I was young and invariably, these would be spent at my aunty and uncle's house in Morden. My mum had grown up in that house and her dad, my granddad, still lived there with his son, my much-loved Uncle John, his wife, Aunty Joan, and my only cousin, Susan. Encompassed in that little house were all the people I loved best in the world apart from my own family, so you can imagine my great sense of joyous anticipation as the Christmas holidays approached.

As we did not own a car, we would travel to Morden on the number 164 bus a few days before Christmas. We would be extremely well-laden, for not only were there suitcases and presents to carry, but also some groceries to add to the feast. For us children it was a time of enormous excitement, but for our parents, particularly Mum, it must have been an awful burden that sorely tried her patience. The bus stop was a twenty minute walk from home, the wintry weather was usually pretty grim, and the company of three fractious children could hardly have been anyone's ideal way of starting their holidays.

Once aboard the bus, however, things became a little more comfortable and the hour-long journey passed quickly.

We sat in the front seat upstairs, pretending to drive the bus, chatting away to any seemingly friendly passengers, or just admiring the exotic and festive sights of Banstead, Sutton, and Rosehill as we passed through.

For me, there was often the added indignity of being forced to spend much of the journey on the conductor's platform due to my uncontrollable travel sickness. This debilitating and anti-social sickness continued to cloud my life until I was eighteen and began to drive myself, whence it miraculously disappeared, only to still return on occasions when I am a passenger in a vehicle being driven recklessly by someone who imagines they are a rally driver.

But, to return to Christmas. Upon reaching our destination, it was as if the magical day had already arrived. It would be late afternoon by then, getting dark, and Morden seemed to us country children like a great, shining metropolis. The Underground station was bustling, the stores were packed with shoppers, and outside the cinema was a beautiful crib and manager from the depths of which came taped recordings of Christmas carols. I have always adored hymns and carols of any kind, so I would insist that we be allowed to crowd around this for a few minutes, soaking up the joyous atmosphere.

From there, it was a short, ten-minute walk to the house, and having reached the top of the road, we children were allowed to race on ahead.

Even today, so many years on, I can still remember the tremendous thrill and exhilaration at knocking on that well-loved front door. After a while it would be gingerly opened by my dear Uncle John, who, upon spotting us, would teasingly refuse entry on the grounds that we were "perishing nuisances." We would laughingly plead that "honestly we weren't" and try to sneak in under his arms, but he would relent only once Mum was safely inside the front gate too.

Once inside the house, our holiday would truly begin. The kettle would be put on to boil, coats and hats taken off and hung up in the narrow hallway, and slippers placed onto our cold, weary feet. On the maternal side of my family, we have always suffered to varying degrees with our feet!

Aunty Joan would usually be in the tiny kitchen when we arrived, making yet another batch of her delicious mince pies and sausage rolls. What a thrill to be allowed to stand there in the warmth of the cosy room, mentally planning exactly how many you would be able to eat before the holiday was over.

Cousin Susan was very useful in this regard, as having witnessed the entire baking process, she could reliably inform me or any other interested party as to the exact number available for consumption.

Christmas Eve was always a very special day, as this is when we did most of our present shopping. Under the supervision of Susan, who was very grown up, being 18 months older than me, we would set off.

The shops in Morden seemed so exciting and sophisticated compared to those in Tadworth. The huge Co-Op store was like an Aladdin's cave. Here, I had no trouble finding suitable gifts; the wooden counters were full of bath cubes, hankies, socks, diaries, and combs galore. I was even able to purchase the annually required box of Turkish Delight for my granddad. Susan was always very helpful with advice on the more difficult decisions, like colour and size. To buy my only uncle the wrong colour comb would have been a tragedy.

My money was soon spent, as unfortunately I was not blessed with the same financial sense as my sister, Carol. She would go Christmas shopping with 2s6d, buy all her presents, and still return home with change. No wonder she has made such a success of her career in banking.

Having spent all our available pocket money, the next treat was riding up and down on the store escalators. For Susan this was a rather boring, mundane exercise, as she was quite cosmopolitan and well used to such things, but for us it was a wonderful adventure, as the only other time we had ridden on a "moving staircase" was on an occasional trip on the London Underground.

Once we eventually got home with all our parcels, there would be a great flurry of activity, as everyone locked themselves away to wrap them up. Invariably, there would be occasional shouts of anguish, from someone who had run out of paper, or Sellotape, but Susan would come to the rescue, as she had always been organised enough to have all her shopping and wrapping done well in advance. After all the hard work, there was the excitement of placing everything under the tree and casually squeezing any parcels that were labelled with your name.

Like most children, we always had great difficulty going to sleep on Christmas Eve, hoping that by staying awake long enough we would catch a glimpse of Father Christmas. I would share Susan's bedroom and we would lie there, discussing at some length, the treasures we expected to find under the tree. I have always believed in overestimating my requirements on a present list, on the assumption that you are unlikely to get at least half. My list below, from Christmas 1963 when I was 12 years old, is fairly typical:

Dear Father Christmas, This is what I want for Christmas please:

Chiffon scarf
Quilted nylon dressing gown
Set undies
Pair best shoes
Beatles LP (Please Please Me)
Pinafore dress
Pair royal blue slacks (from Marks)
Petticoat (stiff)
TV Stars and Singers Annual
Chiffon scarf
Puzzle book
Pleated skirt
Some sweets, etc.

I can't remember what items from this comprehensive list I was lucky enough to receive, but I think I definitely deserved the chiffon scarf (mentioned twice) solely based on my persistence.

Waking early on Christmas Day was exquisite pain because we knew it would be hours before we could open our presents.

It had become, over the years, an unspoken rule that we all had to be washed and dressed before the excitement could begin. In theory this was reasonable enough, even to our impatient little minds, except for one slight flaw… Granddad.

We were not allowed to begin until he arrived downstairs, and then we had to wait an interminable amount of time for him to wash and shave. He was a lovely man, but certainly not above a bit of good-humoured teasing of his grandchildren. I am quite sure that he used to lie in bed, drinking his early morning cup of tea - which one of us had delivered in the hope of speeding him up a little - chuckling to himself as he heard our grumbles. Finally, just when we were beginning to give up hope of ever opening our presents, he would come shakily down the stairs, the teacup and saucer rattling in his bony old hands. We watched, absolutely fascinated, as he shaved the white bristles on his chin with a scary-looking, cut-throat razor. He would then potter about for a few minutes more before finally conceding that he was ready and festivities could now begin.

He liked to distribute his gifts first.

Every year, for as long as I can remember, these were exactly the same. There was a brown envelope for each of us (adults included) with our names written in his spidery old hand. Inside each envelope was a ten shilling note. This money was to be used to buy either a new pair of slippers or a length of material to make a new dress. Because he was such a caring man, he realised that hard cash soon lost its novelty for small children, so the envelope also contained a 6d bar of Cadbury's milk chocolate.

Then there remained the pile of presents under the tree. With enormous enjoyment, Uncle John would dispatch these to their new owners amid squeals of delight. Finally, to our great disappointment, everything was gone, but we as individuals were greatly enriched by the whole process and were now the proud owners of wonders unlimited. Looking back, the gifts we received were tiny and inexpensive in comparison to what children now expect, but at the time we were more than happy with our lot.

Whilst the grownups disappeared into the kitchen to prepare the lunch and enjoy a much-needed and reviving cup of tea, we children would spend a very happy hour or two comparing our goodies and sampling the delights of our Cadbury's selection boxes.

Needless to say, this never appeared to spoil our appetites for lunch, my favourite of which was the dessert: Christmas pudding, mince pies, custard, and thick, thick, cream, all mixed together to make anyone's mouth water!

After lunch we would all collapse for an hour or so until we were feeling a little less full; then it was time to sing and dance and play Housey Housey (Bingo), Draughts, or word guessing games like, "name ten flowers beginning with the letter 'S.'"

Sometimes Susan and I, as the eldest of the children, would give impromptu performances - renditions of Perry Como's "Catch a Falling Star" or the ever-popular "How Much is that Doggy in the Window," complete with full theatrical actions. We loved the Lonnie Donogan song, "My Old Man's a Dustman," especially the bit "he wears cor blimey trousers and lives in a council flat." Mum would never let us use the word "blimey" at home as she considered it swearing, but when her beloved brother was encouraging his nieces and nephews to sing along, she had to grin and bear it. In her whole life, I only ever heard my Mum swear twice; usually she would just say, "Oh BBC," if she was really cross.

On one memorable Christmas, Uncle John taught me to do the Twist, Chubby Checker style, by imagining I was drying my back with a towel. I dare you to try it.

A few days after the celebrations, my family would return to Tadworth and I would be invited to stay on with my cousin for another week or so.

What a wonderful time I used to have.

Susan was an only child, and therefore much more used to the material things in life, like baked beans on toast at a Lyons Corner House followed by a trip to the cinema to see a Norman Wisdom film. There were shopping trips to the West End, Wimbledon, Tooting, and Putney, and I would return home at the end of my stay feeling very grown up and worldly.

Susan. My only cousin and best counterpart for so many years. We were close, more like sisters - enemies one minute, bosom pals the next. She was such a big part of my childhood; I wore her outgrown clothes, absorbed many of her opinions and ideas, and read all her old comics. Sometimes, she and Uncle John would come to Tadworth to visit us, bringing a whole suitcase full of clothes and old Judy and Bunty comics. After the pair had left, I would retire to the bedroom to drown myself in the new material, in absolute bliss.

Because of my friendship with Marilyn - she of the Primary School sickness incident - I gained lots of new experiences. She was a lovely girl, another only child, who lived in a really nice house near the Downs, with an enormous garden. Her parents were lovely, really kind to me, despite the fact that I didn't come from a family as affluent as theirs.

They organised the most wonderful birthday parties with treasure hunts and presents hidden in the trees and bushes. At their home, I tried coffee cake, learnt how to use toenail clippers, and slept alone in a bedroom for the first time in my life.

I also learnt to cope with real disappointment through my friendship with Marilyn.

Her parents had invited me to stay for a whole weekend and we planned to sleep in a tent in her garden, and then go to the cinema in Epsom to see the Disney film "Dumbo."

I had been desperate to have a baby elephant as a pet for years and, on my fifth birthday, was bitterly disappointed when I received a blue budgerigar instead - a cute little chap that I called, Joey. I loved him, but couldn't understand my parents' reasoning that a baby elephant was not a suitable pet. After all, we had a garden!

Anyway, I had been looking forward to the Dumbo adventure for weeks and when the great day finally dawned, I awoke quite early in the morning. Sadly however, one look in the mirror spoke volumes. I was covered in spots and had obviously caught the chicken pox that was making its rounds of the neighbourhood. Undeterred, I washed and dressed in preparation for my outing, but of course as soon as Mum caught sight of me that was out of the question. I begged and pleaded to no avail and ended up screaming at her, saying that she was mean and nasty and never wanted me to have a good time. Needless to say many, many years passed before I finally got to see the Dumbo movie, as there were no DVDs or video rental shops in those days.

Another friend from primary school, Frances, lived in a big house on the same street as Marilyn. She also held parties in her garden, although we really preferred to be invited into her bedroom to play as she had some wonderful treasures. I was particularly envious of her foreign doll collection, which included a rather splendid set of Russian stacking dolls. These had apparently been a gift from Premier Khrushchev, as her father was Frank Cousins, the trade unionist.

When I was a little older, I became a Saturday morning picture kid.

There used to be two cinemas in Epsom, The Odeon near the Clock House, which had a fish and chip shop right next door, and the Granada at the other end of the High Street.

We favoured the Odeon. For the princely sum of a few old pence, you could sit in the plush, red seats and be entertained for a whole morning. The only commitment required from the audience was to stand up for the National Anthem and then sing along to the club song "We come along on Saturday mornings, greeting everybody with a smile." Further noisy renditions of this on the bus home often caused a problem or two with the kids who supported the Granada. Although no one actually ever came to blows, there was little love lost between the opposing camps. Sadly, both cinemas are long gone, the Odeon having made way for a Sainsbury's supermarket and so the delicious smell of frying chips is lost forever, buried under concrete and metal stands full of healthy vegetables.

THE CAMPAIGNERS

When I was six years old, I had a great desire to join *something*. Anything would do; I just wanted to be part of something.

As we lived very close to the Marbles Way Junior School, which was used on Sundays by the local evangelical church, it was decided I should try there.

Within a very short space of time I came to love going there to Sunday school and eventually, I joined the youth movement attached to the church known as the "Campaigners." This movement consisted of three basic sections: Junos, Inters, and Craftsmen, and in my time, I became an enthusiastic member of them all.

Initially, I attended Junos every Monday evening wearing my green uniform and feeling very special, between the hours of 6.30 and 7.30. We were kept very well occupied with the learning of new skills, such as knot tying, shoe shining, astronomy, semaphore and Morse code, as well as silver polishing, window cleaning, bible reading, shopping, and learning to use a telephone box - a very necessary skill in those long ago days before mobile phones were invented. All these things were aimed to help us develop and grow into useful members of society. As we progressed through the ranks the tasks became more difficult, but they were always fun and the whole ordeal certainly added a very enjoyable facet to my early life. Additionally, we played lots of team games, which often became very competitive to instill a sense of loyalty in us too.

In Junos, we would give regular displays of our new skills to our families, and of course we looked forward to showing off. Our group leaders were all quite inventive and we gave some very memorable performances. I recall one in particular, a rendition of the popular song, "Oh soldier, soldier won't you marry me?" which we thoroughly enjoyed, as it meant dressing up in beautiful costumes as either the soldier or his sweet maid. As there were about 20 of us in the group, it must have taken some pretty intensive sewing to make all the outfits; every time we did a show it involved a lot of costume changes, and I now realise just how dedicated those leaders must have been, for they were all volunteers! I truly admire them still, for I am fairly sure that filling every Monday evening with twenty or so noisy and excitable little girls would not be everyone's idea of heaven.

When I was nine, a whole new world opened up to me thanks to the Campaigners. I was invited to go to summer camp, and as we had never been able to afford family holidays, it was decided that somehow we would scrape together the six pounds six shillings required to send me to Great Yarmouth for a week's camping.

Camping does not really describe the experience, for when we children arrived we discovered that we were to sleep in a boarding school dormitory. This was even more exciting than camping in a boring old tent, as it meant no insects and no problems if it rained. Also, it was going to be much nicer having our long-planned midnight feasts sitting up in a nice warm bed. If we felt an overwhelming desire to see the stars, we could always stick our heads out of the dormitory windows.

I have not returned to Great Yarmouth since and hope I never shall, because I would hate to destroy the wonderful memories I have of the place.

We arrived on a Saturday afternoon and spent the rest of the day exploring our new surroundings. It was tremendously exciting to meet so many new people; in all there were about one hundred little girls from various parts of the country.

I found the whole experience completely intoxicating.

That first night, several of us cried ourselves to sleep, not because we were really homesick, but because at the tender age of nine, we were suddenly confronted with communal living. It was going to take a bit of getting used to.

The next morning we woke early, and after making our beds and dressing in our smart green uniforms, we went into the huge dining room for breakfast.

The food was excellent and for the first time in my life, I tasted tinned tomatoes on toast. I loved them so much that after that, I had them every morning for the whole week of our stay.

After breakfast, we took a stroll to the local church; they had been warned in advance of our arrival. As we approached the old stone church we began marching in our smartest manner: left, right, left, right. Drill was another skill we had been taught on Monday evenings.

One lucky, but rather frightened girl marched at the front carrying our clan colours (our flag) proudly. To carry the colours at Church Parade in your own parish was one thing, but here there was a strange vicar and an inquisitive congregation to worry about. Over the next few years, wherever we went to camp, the local churches always took us completely in their stride; I think they rather enjoyed the spectacle of dozens of little girls smartly uniformed and trying desperately not to let their halos slip.

After the church service, we were dismissed and returned to camp for lunch. As it was Sunday and we were a church organisation, it was not deemed suitable for us to go wandering around the town, so we would head off to the beach for sand competitions. Again, it was all team work, and we would all vie to make the best possible bible texts in the sand. The old favourites always appeared: "Thy word is a lamp unto my feet" being particularly good, as there is plenty of scope for sand drawings of lamps, feet, and paths. This vying for holiness would keep us occupied for most of the afternoon, and by the time we returned to camp for tea, almost the whole beach would be covered in bible texts. I often look back and wonder how many holidaymakers had a good chuckle as they took their late afternoon strolls and were confronted with such religious enthusiasm.

The rest of the week passed in a flurry of excitement, with lots of midnight feasts - both organised and illicit - visits to the waxworks, flower clock gardens, and boating lakes. By the time Friday came, we were all beginning to wish that our holiday could go on forever; the prospect of being parted from our new friends was quite distressing. But duty must come first, and so we spent our final day shopping for presents for our families. We were allowed to take pocket money to camp, but only a small amount. It had to last all week *and* buy our souvenirs. We had a tuck shop, but fortunately our leaders - or chiefs, as they were known - strictly limited the amount we could spend in any one day at this haven of delight. This was just as well, as I have always had an insatiable penchant for chocolate.

Their rules meant we still had a respectable amount of money left by Friday to purchase the necessary gifts. It was a tremendous worry though, and caused me a lot of heartache. Should I be really generous and spend every remaining penny on my beloved family? Or should I keep back a little to buy myself another chocolate bar?

Such momentous decisions required me to spend at least an hour in Woolworths. Would Mum and Dad like a cruet set, embellished with the name of the seaside town, or some vanilla fudge in a pretty box? A few sticks of rock, or a little wooden plaque that said "With love from Great Yarmouth"? My siblings were easy to satisfy; a couple of sticks of pink rock would suffice for them. In the end, for Mum and Dad, I settled on a rather splendid cruet set in the shape of an ocean liner, with salt and pepper pots as the funnels.

Saturday dawned and we rose early to begin our long journey home. Tearful goodbyes were said, together with promises to meet again at Camp Reunion in London the following November.

It is difficult to be sad for long though, when you are just nine years old and have suddenly discovered that the world is a big and exciting place. The return journey was spent happily reminiscing about our wonderful holiday on the train, while frequently being given stern warnings from our chiefs about sticking our heads out of the open window. If we did not pull our heads in, they would certainly be chopped off by a passing express train.

Once we changed trains in London and were safely installed on the last lap of our journey, my thoughts turned to Tadworth and my dear family. I suddenly realised just how much I had missed them; I could hardly contain myself as the train finally pulled into the station and I saw Mum waiting for me on the platform.

None of these loving caring thoughts transmitted as far as her ears though, for as soon as I stepped off the train, looking to her horror as though I hadn't combed my hair or washed my face for the whole week, the first words I apparently uttered were "I had a wonderful time; can I please go again next year?"

Go again next year I certainly did, and for several years thereafter. The novelty never wore off.

For the next three or four years we went to the Isle of Wight, just off the south coast of England, and stayed in a lovely old school called Little Appley at Seaview, just outside Ryde. This was a boys boarding school, which had very large grounds with peacocks, cricket pitches, and an old underground bomb shelter. One day we decided to try this particular spot for size, although of course, it was strictly out of bounds. It proved easy to crawl into, but was really horrid, dark, cold, and cramped, and I felt such sympathy for those poor wartime schoolboys who had been forced to use it.

The Isle of Wight was quaint and much quieter than the mainland with so much for little girls to see and do. We scrambled up the cliffs in Alum Bay to collect our own coloured sand (sadly this is no longer possible in these days of health and safety restrictions), we visited the Needles, Blackgang Chine, Carisbrooke Castle, the boating lake at Ryde, and the beaches at Seaview, Sandown, and Shanklin.

My world became so much wider because of my wonderful summer camp experiences, and I began to see a quite different side to life and people. At one of these camps I met a truly remarkable lady. She was a missionary and had just escaped from the Belgian Congo troubles, and although she obviously censored her stories to be suitable for young and impressionable ears, my imagination was well and truly stirred and for quite a long time afterwards I longed to become a missionary myself. In retrospect, I can see that I am far too fond of my creature comforts to ever have been suitable missionary material, but at that time, my idealism ran high and I could see no boundaries.

The final summer camp I attended proved to be differently memorable than the others. I was fifteen by then, and at that age it was deemed suitable for us girls to finally share our holidays with the opposite sex. We had been mixing for some time at our own clan level, but most of the boys in our clan we had known since primary school so we judged them harshly as not-necessarily-ideal specimens of manhood. Oh, what bliss this mixed camp promised, and for several months our holiday wardrobes were carefully planned to include the most suitable items of clothing.

This camp was to be held at Seaford College in Sussex, another boarding school vacated by its usual pupils for the summer holiday. As there were only ten of us going - five boys and five girls - we travelled by minibus rather than train. It was a fairly short journey, so we didn't leave until just before midday. By the time we arrived, most of the other campers were already installed. To our absolute delight there were several delicious-looking boys, the most attractive ones coming from Bolton in Lancashire. We could hardly contain our excitement. However, it was to be remarkably short-lived.

Having barely unpacked, the boys from our group suddenly disappeared. We were well segregated, with separate bedrooms for boys and girls on opposite sides of the landing. However, our boys were quite protective and usually felt obliged to keep us informed of their whereabouts in case we should need them.

We finished our unpacking as quickly as possible, and, having changed into something suitably seductive (if I recall correctly, a blue lacy top and navy blue stretch nylon slacks), we made our way downstairs, fully expecting to be greeted with rapturous cries of welcome from those divine "Bolton Boys."

Well, they do say you only learn by your own experiences, and we certainly learnt a lesson that day. Unbeknown to us *mere* females, it just happened to be the most important day in that decade of footballing history. 30thJuly 1966 - the day England won the World Cup.

All those very desirable young men were slouched around the television set, watching the match. I don't think any of us girls had prepared for such a formidable opponent; five very dejected fifteen year olds wandered into the garden with disappointment written all over our faces. And guess what we found? Yes, quite right, another twenty or so girls, all done up to the nines and no-one to do it with. Still, it made a great topic of conversation to break the ice with new friends, and in no time at all we had become *women of the world*, completely understanding of male weaknesses.

By the time the match was eventually over and duly won and the boys emerged into the late afternoon sunshine, we girls were all great friends and comrades, feeling sufficiently martyred to agree to join in the suggested re-enactment of the exciting game.

One enjoyable facet of the football craze that touched so heavily on our lives that summer was the supporters song that the boys condescendingly taught to us. To this day I can still sing along to those memorable lyrics, "We've got Gordon Banks in the goal, Gordon Banks in the goal."

I would hate you to think that my first real social encounter with the opposite sex was less than fun. The rest of the holiday was absolutely fantastic. Those good-looking boys proved to be just as much fun as we hoped and we had a great time, doing lots of silly, innocent things that young teenagers enjoy. Because we were primarily a church group there was a lot of emphasis on faith, but that just enhanced everything. It was so nice to know that these boys would not laugh at us for going to church, but that they actually shared our beliefs.

There was, eventually, great sadness at our partings, but now, with increased maturity we realised that Bolton was not at the end of the world and that there would be every opportunity to continue our friendship.

As I have previously mentioned, I was lucky enough to be blessed with a very optimistic nature and consequently viewed every new experience with great delight. Even seemingly ordinary events took on an added splendour in my mind.

When our primary school teacher, Miss Truss, recounted her experiences of learning to use chopsticks in a Chinese restaurant, I was enthralled. Of course in these days of takeaways that sounds terribly commonplace, but at that time in the 1950s, it seemed to me like a great adventure. How I longed to go to mainland China and try chopsticks out for myself.

I was always an avid reader, and until they built the new library at Tattenham Corner I was more than happy to visit the mobile library that came to the St. Mark's church hall once a week. The van only had a small children's section, so I quickly outgrew that and sometimes tried to borrow titles from the adults area. The librarians obviously censored my choices, but one book in particular made a huge impact on me. It was about the life of Marie Antoinette, and although I enjoyed reading about her extravagant lifestyle at Versailles, my favourite part was the final page where there was a very graphic account of her beheading at the guillotine. I must have read and reread that particular page dozens of times!

Memories of my friend Lorraine are markers of my growing adolescence. She lived opposite me, in one of the houses my mum so admired, with the large picture windows overlooking the street. She was two years my senior, an only child, and she attended a private girls school in Sutton. Mum considered her to be a suitable companion, so we spent many hours lounging in her bedroom listening to Radio Luxembourg and a man called Horace Batchelor, who tried to persuade you to enter the Irish Sweepstake merely by phoning a Keynsham, Bristol number. Obviously he was a forerunner to the hard-sell, cold-calling scams of today.

We would spend ages painting our nails with Cutex Pearl Pink or colourless nail varnish whilst discussing the current Top Ten hits. When carrying on in this decadent manner, we would eat delicious homemade Scottish shortbread, sandwiched together with strawberry ice cream.

I always assumed that her parents were terribly rich because they owned a car - a Hillman Minx - and sent Lorraine to a fee-paying school where she played lacrosse. Mrs. Parker, her mother, would get her groceries delivered to the house. Obviously this was long before the days of internet shopping, so it seemed to be a big deal to me.

With Lorraine, I attended the Phoenix Youth Club a few times. Although I would never have admitted it, I actually found it pretty intimidating, as all the others seemed very grown up and much more worldly than me. We would all sit outside on the swings and I would watch in awe as Lorraine flirted with some of the big, scary boys. We would usually be wearing our trendy, chunky jumpers and pleated skirts; mine were handed down from Lorraine and I was thrilled to have them. She was also lucky enough to own a "Dr. Kildare" shirt, and as the actor Richard Chamberlain who played the Kildare character was quite a heartthrob of ours at the time, I was wildly jealous - especially when she would put it on every time we listened to his recordings of "Hi Lili, Hi Lo" and "All I Have to Do is Dream."

When we were much younger, we had been more than satisfied playing outside with the other kids in the street. As there were almost no cars passing down our road, we could indulge in games of hide-and-seek in the bushes, "Queenie, Queenie, who's got the Ball," "What's the time Mr. Wolf," or skipping with a long rope tied between two lamp posts. We established camps in the fields behind our houses, with a suitable tree stump as storage for our supply of dock leaves. These were vital to alleviate the pain of nettle rash.

As we grew, so did our desire for more adult pleasures. What bliss to be allowed to spend a day in London all on our own. I was just eleven the first time the two of us went, but felt extremely sophisticated as we made our way by bus and underground around the capital. We visited the Victoria and Albert Museum and spent ages in the costume department, imagining ourselves as Victorian beauties. Then we climbed the three hundred and eleven steps of the Monument and peered out from the very top, imagining the Great Fire of London of 1666, which it had been built to commemorate.

After all that culture, we then repaired to the Wimpy Bar at Charing Cross, where we each devoured two hamburgers and a glass of milk. This was my first experience of junk food, and I am not ashamed to confess that I still indulge in a hamburger on occasion. However, I will never, ever forget that *first* taste.

I went ice-skating a few times with Lorraine at Silver Blades rink in Streatham. I was a lousy skater - far too nervous of falling and getting my fingers chopped off - but I loved to go into the rink café afterwards for a plate of chips. We would travel to Streatham by train and sometimes get off in Sutton to wander up and down the High Street, stopping off at Lyons Corner House for a bowl of tomato soup and a crusty roll with butter. This particular café was opposite a large department store called Shinner's, and I remember the day of

Winston Churchill's funeral when the shop windows were draped in black and all the shops closed for an hour as a sign of respect.

Although I considered Lorraine and myself to be "best friends," sometimes she would, of course, spend time with girls from her school. On these occasions, I would feel rather unwanted and left out. I tried not to let this peevishness show too much, and occasionally I would be included in their outings.

One day, Mrs. Parker asked if I would be interested in using Lorraine's ticket to attend the Searchers concert at the Granada cinema in Sutton, as she was unwell and couldn't go. I was elated even though I wasn't a particular fan of that group, and I set off in high spirits.

Lorraine's friend and her mother (neither of whom I had ever met before) met me off the bus and we were dropped at the cinema with the strict instruction that we were to be back outside and ready to be picked up, the *minute* the concert was over. The first act was a singer called Eden Kane. He was dressed all in black, with just a white tie to add some colour and his gyrating on stage caused the screaming to start. Mass hysteria is quite something, and I found myself screaming out with the rest of the audience when the Searchers finally appeared. I was quite exhausted when the concert finally ended, but along with a few other girls, we decided to try and track the group down. Forgetting that our lift awaited us, we climbed fire escapes and peered into empty windows. We were becoming quite desperate, until the manager of the cinema came out and said that if we left our autograph books, he would ensure they were signed by our heroes. True to his word, I still have those autographs.

Lorraine and I, like most girls in the Sixties, adored the Beatles and would spend hours listening to their records and discussing their various attributes. She was lucky enough to own all their LPs. Lorraine loved John Lennon, whilst my passion was solely for Paul McCartney. I was so envious when she went to see them at the Hammersmith Odeon. The tickets were far too expensive for me, but I did have a Beatles-style haircut much to my great-aunt Rose's distress. She considered it very unladylike, and couldn't understand why my mother had allowed such a thing. I saved some coupons and sent away for a cereal bowl - which Mum approved of as it encouraged me to eat my breakfast quickly - so that I could uncover the Beatles' faces smiling at me from the bottom of the bowl.

For many years, Lorraine and I had a standing arrangement to swap comics. We were each allowed one a fortnight, and in the early days these were "Princess" or "Judy." As we became teenagers however, our tastes veered more towards "Fabulous" or "New Musical Express."

Lorraine and her family were great travellers, and I still have lots of postcards that she sent me over the years. Never did I imagine that one day, places like Westward Ho, Dartmouth, York, and Paris would become as familiar to me as they seemed to her. Each year they would set off for Ayrshire for Hogmanay (New Year's Eve), and I loved to hear about the swishing kilts and gallons of whisky consumed.

Mrs. Parker was a Scot and the family decided to move back to Scotland when I was fourteen. I cried so much when Lorraine and I said our farewells.

We tried to keep in touch, but it was much harder in the days before texting, emails, and Facebook, and I didn't have a telephone at home.

The last I heard from her, more than fifty years ago, was when she wrote to tell me that she was marrying a Scots lad called Sandy. I now realise how important it is to keep in contact with all your friends, but I guess that is wisdom gained in maturity; it was certainly not something I possessed in my late teens.

Growing up, I saw very little of my dad's parents. They only lived an hour away, but sadly Mum had a rather strained relationship with

them, so she kept them at arms-length from her children. At the time I didn't understand any of this; I never questioned why they were never invited to spend Christmas or birthdays with us, or why I only remember spending one, delightful night sleeping over at their house. Once I was grown up I tried to see them more often, but as a busy teenager with precious little time to spare for elderly relatives, it never occurred to me that they wouldn't be around forever.

I now realise that it must have been pretty heartbreaking for them too. After all, I was their eldest grandchild and I had spent the first three years of my life living in their house. Dad was a good son and visited them weekly, and on the odd occasions when Mum allowed us to go along too, they seemed delighted to see us. Granddad would always put a shiny half crown in our hands as we left. They were Cockneys, Londoners born and bred and both came from large families, but because of the situation, I never met any of my extended paternal family.

This is a great sadness to me, as although I was brought up to believe that they were not particularly nice people, I now realise that while I have many of Mum's good traits, I am also very much like my dad and his parents. By the time I was thirty years old they had both died, leaving me no links to the other side of my family other than some old sepia photos. Hopefully Ancestry.com will be able to fill in a few of the gaps for me.

GROWING UP, LOVE, CLOTHES, AND FUN

Reaching puberty was a very difficult time for me. Not because I hated the changes in my body, but because they couldn't happen quickly enough. By the time I was 14, most of the other girls in my class at school had already started to mature and develop a bust while the only thing I was developing was desperation. In the end, I pretended that nature had taken its course, but keeping up the pretence of a sprouting bosom was a little difficult. Cotton wool was a great help, as were the fashionable conical padded bras, but oh, the humiliation, when another girl in the school changing room announced that it was all false and everyone discovered my flat chest.

Another little problem arose when I was invited to a school friend's birthday party. During discussions beforehand on what to wear to the great event, it became apparent that all my peers would be fashionably dressed - up to the nines.

To prove that I was just as grown up as them, I agreed that yes, of course, I too would be wearing my stockings and suspenders. This was despite the fact that at the ripe old age of thirteen, I only possessed long white socks, far too childish for the image I required. Some fast thinking was needed.

As soon as Lorraine arrived home from school, I rushed over and explained my predicament. She was astute enough to realise that this little deception had to be kept secret; after all, if my mum had felt

I was old enough to wear stockings, there would not be a problem. This was way before the days of tights (pantyhose).

So, Lorraine lent me one of her suspender belts and a brand new pair of American Tan stockings, delivered together with a quick lesson on how to wear them. Also included in the kit was a bottle of the aforementioned Cutex nail varnish, in case of ladders.

The next afternoon I left home looking like a sweet schoolgirl in my long white socks, only to hide in the bushes on my way to the bus stop and emerge feeling extremely sophisticated, modelling American Tan stockings.

The only flaw in my little plan came later in the evening when my dad arrived to collect me from the party. As I have already mentioned, we never owned a car and travelled everywhere by bus or foot, so we were thrilled when another parent offered us a lift home rather than having to wait for ages at a cold, draughty bus stop.

It had been such a lovely party - just girls and soft drinks - but quite intoxicating nonetheless, and in my excitement I had completely forgotten about the stockings. Mum, of course, spotted them the minute I walked in the door and gently enquired as to their origins. When I tearfully explained, she told me what a silly girl I was and that if she had realised how important it was to me, she would have let me wear them for such a special occasion. She promised that I could start wearing them regularly once I was 14 and true to her word, on my next birthday, one of my parcels contained a pretty suspender belt and a pair of stockings. I proudly wore them to school that very day and was thrilled when everyone noticed… and a few boys pinged my suspenders!

It seems strange to write it now, but back in the 1950s and 60s there seemed to be much more innocence (or perhaps, ignorance), and sex was certainly not a word that was bandied around lightly. There was censorship in newspapers and on television, and girlie magazines like Playboy were not readily available in newsagents except on the top shelf where small people couldn't reach them.

My mum didn't tell me anything to prepare me for becoming a young woman, but once opened the drawer in her dressing table, pointed out a little parcel wrapped in tissue paper, and told me I "would need that one day." I had absolutely no idea what she was talking about, but didn't question her further.

I heard lots of rumours in the playground at school of course, but they seemed incomprehensible to me and in our biology lessons we only learnt about the reproduction of rabbits, which truthfully wasn't terribly helpful.

I had recently had a very unpleasant experience, when playing ball with my little sister on Epsom Downs. I had thrown the ball a bit too hard and it had gone into some thick bushes. As I walked over to retrieve it, a man came out carrying my ball in one hand. In the other he held himself, his trousers were open, exposing his manhood. Luckily my little sister was too far away to see him, so I grabbed her and we ran away as fast as we could. Stupidly, I never told anyone, but that vision has stayed with me forever. Until that day, I had never seen a naked man. My dad, apart from having a rather eccentric penchant for shorts even in the height of winter, was always suitably dressed, even when in his pyjamas.

Naturally, I was desperate to know more. By this time Lorraine had moved to Scotland, and anyway I am not sure if I would ever have felt comfortable asking her about such personal things. So instead, I wrote to Evelyn Home, the agony aunt in a women's magazine, asking if she could tell me the facts of life!

Unfortunately, I couldn't afford to buy a stamp, so I hid the envelope under my pillow and was waiting until the weekend when I would get my pocket money.

When I arrived home from school one afternoon that week, Mum was waiting. She had found the letter when she changed my bedsheets. She was obviously very upset that I was writing to a stranger for advice, but was so embarrassed that she still couldn't bring herself to discuss my questions with me. Instead, she gave me a stamp to post the letter. Eventually, I got a reply, a photocopied couple of pages entitled "Growing up for girls and boys." It gave me the basic idea in a very cold and clinical way, and Mum never felt able to elaborate on my knowledge, other than to tell me that I "must never get into trouble." For a very long time however, I had absolutely no idea what she meant by that. It was only a few years later that I realized when a girl down the road got pregnant before marriage. How times have changed since then!

Another excellent source of "grown-up" clothing came about quite unexpectedly. Once we three children were all happily installed at primary school, Mum decided it was time for her to return to work. Obviously, being such a devoted mother, she wanted to be around whenever we needed her, and this limited her choices. She was offered a job cleaning a large house on Epsom Downs, and because we needed the money she swallowed her pride and accepted it. It was to prove a wise decision, because the house owners, Mr. and Mrs. Crosland, were a charming couple. Over the next few years, we all benefited because of Mum's hard work and their generosity.

Shortly after taking on this job, Mum discovered she was pregnant again. She was very distressed, as she was now over forty and certainly not planning on another baby, but as usual, she coped so well that we children did not realise anything was amiss. Baby Margaret was born at home on a Thursday afternoon, during our favourite children's TV show – Crackerjack. We were allowed to see her when she was just a few minutes old and it was instant love for Carol and me, but our brother Michael was bitterly disappointed at having yet *another* girl in the family.

Just a few weeks after the birth, Mum returned to work and Mrs. Crosland welcomed her and the new baby with open arms. In the school holidays we would all go to work with her and of course, at that time, we had no comprehension of how difficult her life must have been. To have to walk the half-hour journey with three younger children, aged 12, 8, and 6, push a new baby in her pram, then spend her whole morning cleaning *somebody else's* house from top to bottom. We were well-disciplined, and if we did become a little boisterous, a withering glance from Mum soon stopped us in our tracks. Technically, we were allowed the run of the house because Mrs. Crosland thought us "such sweet, well-behaved children," but in practice, Mum would keep a very strict eye on our whereabouts and preferred us in the garden, where there were no valuable antiques to damage.

At Christmas and on our birthdays, the Croslands would give us each a card with a five pound note inside, which was riches untold. For Easter we always received beautiful, expensive Easter eggs and when they travelled to Switzerland each summer to stay with a millionaire friend, we would receive, by parcel post, an enormous box of delicious Swiss chocolates.

The Croslands had a grown-up daughter, Wendy, who was training to be a nurse. I thought she was wonderful, so glamorous and kind. I was absolutely thrilled when I began to inherit her cast-off clothes. Some of my most memorable outfits came from her rejects. Some I can remember include a wonderful little navy blue dress with a red, daisy-cut collar that came from the Renee Shaw boutique in Sutton and a beautiful pink silk halter-neck dress from Switzerland. Mum remodelled the latter into a fashionable mini-dress and a beige knitted dress, which showed off my skinny and flat-chested figure to perfection!

Mum continued to work for them for many years, until Mr. Crosland died unexpectedly and Mrs. Crosland sold up and moved away. She then passed shortly after. This was a very sad loss, particularly for Mum, as she had grown very fond of the two over the years.

At the age of three, I fell in love for the first time. It was with Ian, the boy next door. He was five and seemed so grown up and knowledgeable; I longed for him to notice me. He was kind in a distant, brotherly fashion, and when not otherwise engaged with his friends in a serious game of marbles or sailing toy boats in puddles, he would sometimes take the time to play with me.

He remained my hero for many years until my tastes changed and I began to look for more excitement in life. But at that time, if I spotted him out in his garden I would casually announce the need for fresh air and disappear outside like a shot, much to the amusement of my parents.

How well I remember the thrill of waking up on the 6th of November every year, for on that day Ian would usually condescend to play "firework shops" with me.

We would collect all the discarded firework wrappers we could find; rocket papers were the best, as we knew they could travel quite a distance and it was fun to guess where they had come from. He usually held the coveted position of shopkeeper because he always had a better stock of wrappers. He was an only child and therefore was more indulged than me. I remember one year on Guy Fawkes night when his whole box of fireworks went off accidentally, all at once, in a glorious blaze of colour!

Hollyhock flowers have always been a great favourite of mine, and this stems from an incident when I was just nine or ten years old. One of my best friends was a girl called Marjorie and we had been friends for some years, although this friendship was sorely tested by my behaviour on one particular occasion.

As I have previously mentioned, I was, when young, inclined to bossiness. To this end, I often wagged my finger at people when attempting to instruct them. Unbeknown to me, this had obviously been annoying Marjorie for some time and one day in the school cloakrooms she imitated me, wagging her finger in the same fashion. I became so incensed, particularly when all the other girls started laughing, that the next moment, as her finger wagged in my face, I bit down on it with all my might! Her face was an absolute picture; it certainly wasn't the reaction she had expected. Needless to say, I was in big trouble - escorted off to the headmaster's study for a stern lecture. A few days later I got my comeuppance when Marjorie and another girl threw pepper in my face at lunchtime. But I digress. Back to the hollyhocks.

One day, shortly after the finger incident, Marjorie invited me to her home for tea after school. We always had to be quiet at her house because her dad would be asleep all afternoon. This was my first experience of night shift workers and it seemed very odd to me because in our house, everyone went to bed and got up at normal times. I don't really remember her dad at all, as he was always in bed when I visited, but I think he worked in some kind of plastics factory. Sometimes, if I was in favour, she would bestow on me a plastic key ring or bottle top.

The highlight of any visit, however, was when her elder brother Chris arrived home from school. He was two years older than us, a rather quiet, shy boy, who attended the local grammar school and was the gardener of the family.

On this particular afternoon, just as I was leaving for home, he surprisingly offered to escort me on the 10-minute walk. As we neared my front door, he thrust a newspaper-wrapped parcel into my hands. He explained that it contained hollyhock plants, grown by his own fair hand. He also gave me sage advice on how to care for them. My first ever gift from someone of the opposite sex.

It was hard at times, not having the same luxuries as my friends. This became more noticeable once I left Shawley Way Primary and had to go to the "big school." The big school in question was known as De Burgh County Secondary School and was just over the road from our house. It had been built just a couple of years previously, on the fields and farmland adjoining Burgh Heath.

It had a good reputation, partly due to the fact that it was brand new but also because the headmaster (Mr. Mather) was a Cambridge don who wore his robes every day to wander the school corridors. Parents, who under other circumstances might have sent their off-spring to expensive, fee-paying schools, opted instead to give this new, bilateral establishment a try.

Consequently, I found myself surrounded by children whose families were more wealthy than mine. One girl even came to school in a chauffeur-driven Rolls Royce. All this conspired to make me rather quiet and unconfident. Because I lived just across the road and money was always tight, I went home for lunch rather than paying for school dinners as my new friends did. This also meant that there was precious little time to bond with my new classmates, only serving to increase my shyness.

One day, things came to a head.

After just a few weeks at my new school, I returned from lunch to find my classmates already back at their desks, due to inclement weather. The teacher was absent and in her place, a girl called Angela was pretending to be in charge. She was standing at the front of the class wiping her writing off the blackboard with my raincoat, declaring that was all the rag was fit for. It was probably a bit shabby, having previously belonged to my cousin, but I had been quite proud of my school uniform until that moment. I was heartbroken. I was only eleven years old and it was truly the first time in my life when I realised that being poor was something of which to be ashamed.

Somehow I got through the afternoon, but when I got home I was utterly distraught. Mum gently explained to me that new clothes were not everything; it was what a person was like inside that really counted. To a humiliated young child, that was rather cold comfort. I hated that girl for years.

Looking back, it must have been far worse for Mum, having to watch her beloved eldest daughter suffer such agonies. At that time, there was not enough money for all of us to be kitted out in brand new school uniforms each time we grew; being the eldest, I automatically inherited my cousin Susan's clothes. This was usually a source of great pleasure to me, as she was an only child and had lots of lovely things which I typically viewed with an acquisitive eye and longed for her to outgrow.

Putting aside for a moment my preoccupation with clothes, I must get back to boys.

As I have said, although I was not allowed any proper boyfriends until I was at least sixteen, I did of course take the usual healthy interest in the males around me.

My friend from church, Carole Ross - a lovely girl who was later to die tragically in a car crash while she was still in her teens - had a brother called Brian. He was rather nice, and she reliably informed me that my first-ever Valentine's Day card, given to me when I was just 12, came from him. As I scarcely spoke to him - merely admired from afar - I have no evidence to support this either way.

My next Valentine's card came from a young man called Nigel, again a brother of a friend. In addition to the card he gave me some bubble gum, which I had to give away as it was strictly forbidden by my parents.

Then there was Paul, a very nice lad from school who cycled all the way from Coulsdon to see me one Sunday morning. I was only 13 years old and when he invited me to the cinema that afternoon, I was so embarrassed and shy that I refused him with some feeble excuse and rushed indoors.

How I wish I could meet up with all the boys I hurt unintentionally now that I have the wisdom and maturity of more years. I would love for them to know how very sorry I am for any pain I caused them all those years ago. Growing up for those boys must have been excruciatingly painful, plucking up the courage to ask a girl out only to have her refuse, often through no fault on his part, just pure innocence and fear on hers.

Next, I had a mild crush on one of our teachers. I decided he bore a marked resemblance to Yuri Gagarin, the Russian astronaut, and was therefore worthy of my attention. Years later, long after I had left school, we met again and he invited me out to dinner. We became very good friends and when he left England to work abroad, it was with a promise that when he returned in a year or so, we would discuss marriage. Mum was thrilled. He was charming, worldly wise, and could offer me a nice life far away from just scraping by in a council house. We wrote regularly of course, in the days without mobile phones, but I was young and soon got caught up in the excitement of being a teenager in the 1960s; it was almost a relief when he wrote to tell me that he was marrying a beautiful Ethiopian girl called Mo.

In between all these crushes and passions, I managed to fit in an emergency acute appendix removal. I would not bother to mention this at all, except that it did have some influence on my romantic thoughts at the time.

After the operation I was placed in a side ward with a girl called Pip. I was only 14 and a very immature little thing; she was a rather worldly 16-year-old. I was still in school, but she attended Ewell Technical College and every afternoon, lots of her fellow students would come to visit her. Boys mostly, for she was very pretty and flirtatious. They would sit on our beds, Ivy League come to life, in their striped college scarves. I thought that I must have died and gone to heaven. I was so envious of their lifestyle that I pretended that instead of my hospital pyjamas, I too usually wore very fashionable gear. Imagine then my distress on the day I was discharged when Mum brought in all my nice, ordinary little girl's clothes.

After the first couple of years at De Burgh we were allowed to opt out of certain lessons, and so the two grammar stream classes merged and I found myself with a new set of friends. This began a whole new phase in my life, one which was to last for the rest of my school days and bring me great joy. At last, I felt like I was a member of the "in crowd." It also meant I could give up having to struggle with Latin classes, at which I was hopelessly inept.

This new group of friends consisted of roughly a dozen or so of us. Most of the girls remained the same over the years - Jen Hargreaves, Viv Fitch, Barbara Wakeham, Barbara Sawyer, and Pat Binder, whilst the selection of boys fluctuated according to our current tastes.

Being too young to date properly, it was great fun to just meet up, play music, drink Coke - or even cider on occasion - and enjoy the company of the opposite sex. Later of course, romances blossomed for real, but in the early days it was good just having those boys around as escorts. With them in tow, we were allowed to visit the Derby Day Fair on Epsom Downs and other such delights, previously forbidden without parental chaperones.

Some of us took the romantic thing too seriously. I remember being heartbroken when Barb Sawyer "stole" one young man I fancied, a desirable fourteen-year-old called Graham Tucker, on a school trip to the Fairfield Halls in Croydon to see a production of Richard the Third. Barb and I, after having lost touch for nearly twenty years, became great friends again in our late thirties and she vehemently denies doing this or even having much recollection of the poor chap. At the time I was mortally wounded and very angry with her, but I recovered a few years later when I met him again at a party and he gallantly walked me home at the end of the evening.

I soon became aware of my desire to compete in the fashion stakes with my friends. I was equally aware that my parents were not in a position to assist me in this venture. Therefore, it was time for my great plan to begin in earnest.

After giving the matter due consideration and taking into account my youth, the fact that I was only just fourteen, combined with the need to continue at school and my obvious lack of any suitable experience, I decided to become a papergirl.

I offered my services to the local corner shop, Beechtree Stores, and after some deliberation on their part due to the fact that all my predecessors had been boys, they agreed to give me a week's trial.

For the grand sum of seven shillings and sixpence a week, I worked every morning, including Sundays, delivering papers to houses, flats, and old people's bungalows.

It was pretty hard work and the bag was jolly heavy for a tiny six-stone girl.

I had to borrow my dad's bike as I didn't have one of my own, and so every morning he got up early to lower the saddle for me, then had to raise it again when I got back about eight o'clock, so he could use the bike to go to work.

I hated the bike, the dark mornings (I had to start at 6.30 so I could get home in time to change for school), and the dogs who growled at me. Some of my customers were lovely though, and I used to look forward to greeting them cheerily each morning. It never crossed my mind to give up, even when I was really fed up, trudging around in the rain or the snow. I forced myself to think of all the lovely clothes I was going to be able to buy with my hard-earned wages.

After three weeks, I could afford to buy a navy blue anorak. Then a few weeks later, a fashionable reefer jacket.

There were other compensations too, like the paper boys I encountered on my travels. I became quite smitten with one, and began to time my round to coincide exactly with his. All to no avail I am afraid, as he later became equally smitten with a beauty consultant from Bentalls in Kingston; there was obviously no way I could compete, as the only time he saw me was when I was covered in black newsprint and wearing my brother's balaclava.

After some time, Mr. and Mrs. Munro, the owners of Beechtree Stores, decided that as I was such a good little papergirl, perhaps I would be an equally good asset in the shop. I was offered the chance of a Saturday morning job, weighing and bagging up potatoes. "Not much of a job," I hear you cry, but believe me, after a hard paper round, the thought of spending a further couple of hours weighing potatoes for hard cash, is a very attractive one.

So began my retail career, and I continued to work there long after I finally left school and began to earn a real living.

I just loved working in that little shop; eventually I graduated from weighing the potatoes to filling the shelves, serving at the cheese and bacon counter, and working the cash register. The full-time shop ladies would all spoil me and give me the benefit of their experience and I felt really important in my lilac-coloured nylon overall. Mr. and Mrs Munro were very kind and whenever there was extra work to be done, they always offered it to me, paying me generously.

Soon however, it became obvious that my schoolwork needed extra attention with exams looming. Reluctantly, I had to give up my paper round. I continued with my Saturday job, and in addition often helped on Sundays, at the sweets and cigarettes counter. This part was a real joy at first because I was allowed to eat as many sweets as I liked, but of course, the novelty quickly faded.

For my remaining teenage years, I managed to earn enough to buy some of life's little luxuries so necessary to a young girl: records, clothes, make up, and dance tickets.

Finally came the big event I had been waiting for: My first proper dance.

This auspicious occasion was to be held at the Methodist church hall in Reigate. After the necessary deliberations as to what on earth to wear, Jen and I set off in her father's car.

For once, I really can't remember what exotic outfit I wore, but I do recall Viv rushing up to us in the girls' cloakroom desperate for our opinion of her new "madras check" dress. Obviously, it was a high-fashion occasion.

We danced the night away under the lustful glances of the boys from Reigate Grammar School. One of these young men danced with me and then we went outside to the church gardens to get some fresh air.

He invited me to go to the cinema with him the following week, but, fearful of parental disapproval, I sadly declined.

It was a wonderful evening, with recordings of Chris Montez and Trini Lopez on the turntable playing "The More I See You," "If I Had a Hammer," and other hits of the time. Sadly the evening was over far too quickly; being a church hall, all festivities stopped at eleven-thirty in order for the space (and us) to be decent for the Sabbath. At that time, we were whisked away by Jen's father. If I remember correctly, we were still chatting up a couple of the boys, even as our car was pulling away. Surely a sign of things to come.

According to my mum, when I arrived home my eyes were shining and I was glowing; she was anxious that I had been drinking alcohol. I hadn't been of course, it was just the sheer excitement of feeling like a grown up, desirable young woman!

With my closest friends, I continued to enjoy long summer evenings, listening to the Kinks, The Beatles, the Byrds, and the Rolling Stones and discussing how to ensnare our next male victim. I think we were all still virgins at this point, so it was all pretty harmless talk. I have vivid memories of that time - Jen with her enviable bust and fun fur coat, Barb and her super highly-patterned ski anorak, and Viv and her father feeding me on toast and delicious homemade lemon curd. What funny things we choose to remember.

In the heady days of the 1960s, Jen and I loved to go to London. Our ambition was to be part of the Swinging Sixties scene, but at just fifteen and sixteen years old, we had to be content with strolling along Kings Road Chelsea, visiting the Tate gallery and window shopping on "groovy" Carnaby Street. In black and white op art dresses with our hair cut in Sassoon-style bobs, we blended nicely into the overall scene of Oxford Street. During another period, wearing flowery dresses with our long, flowing hair, bare feet, and bells around our persons, we drifted into India Craft near Marble Arch to buy ethnic jewellery and joss sticks.

When I was fifteen, the school organised a trip to Yugoslavia.

I had never been abroad and knew that family finances would be unable to support such a venture, but mentioned it to Mum nevertheless. You can imagine my delight when she agreed that I could go. Apparently an insurance policy that she had taken out when I was a baby was due to mature and she felt that I would benefit from the holiday. Plans were made and Mum sat up, night after night, sewing dresses and knitting jumpers for me. She was determined that I would be as well-dressed as my friends, and to this day I fondly remember the orange shirt dress and brown chunky cardigan that she laboured over so long.

We caught the boat train from London to Harwich. It was early spring and the crossing to the Hook of Holland was very rough. Once on dry and stable land, we boarded a train that was to take us across Holland, through Germany and Austria, and finally to Yugoslavia.

That train journey was such fun. There were about twenty of us and just four teachers, whom we avoided like the plague. I loved everything about that trip. The hard, black bread and funny sausages we ate, the lack of sleep, and the surly border guards, who mounted the train at each stop and demanded to see our passports.

At one place we dismounted and were shepherded into the huge station restaurant for a meal. There were great tureens of steaming soup and very noisy fellow diners.

The coach whisked us to our hotel in Opatija on the northwest coast. We were the first school party ever to stay at the new, modern hotel, so we were told that we must behave decorously, so as not to offend the management.

I had never stayed in a proper hotel before and absolutely loved the luxury of it all. Despite dire warnings from our teachers, every evening saw us joyriding in the lifts, partying in our bedrooms, and sailing along the corridors in the laundry trolleys.

We were always rather better-behaved in the hotel dining room, as the food was extremely good and the atmosphere tranquil. But most importantly, it was because there was a resident pop group of good-looking Yugoslavs with whom we girls instantly fell in love.

Of course this was primarily an educational trip, so we were taken on lots of excursions to Plitvice lakes, Pula, Split, and the island of Krk. I loved discovering this very different culture, but the best time of all was when we were allowed to explore Opatija town.

We girls were only given leave to explore if we had the chaperonage of the boy pupils, but obviously they did not particularly want to drag us around town with them. However, that little problem was easily solved. They would agree to tell our teachers that they would accompany us, as long as we bought them a bottle of the cheap local wine at the first hostelry we came across. Then we would part ways, them to continue drinking until they felt ill, us to explore the shops and local boys. We very soon realised the latter was not a particularly good idea; while we just wanted a little innocent, romantic interlude, they definitely had something more intense in mind. Boys aside, we had a great time in the shops buying Yugoslav pop records, lace tablecloths and other souvenirs to take home as presents, bottles of cheap wine to drink in our hotel rooms, and the *piece de resistance* – Jen and I each acquired a pair of traditional boots made of white canvas - a little like hockey boots with the toes cut out. We wore these very proudly on our return to England, although quite what we looked like I cannot imagine. Having said that, more than fifty years later the shops are full of very similar-looking boots, so I guess we must have been trendsetters!

Such an exotic taste of foreign places merely served to fuel my wanderlust and I realised then, that whenever my time, finances, and circumstances allowed, I would be off like a shot.

My previously-mentioned desire to work hard and achieve greater status in life was sadly not to be seen in any academic way. I have a theory that mixed-sex schools are excellent for one's social growth but pretty hopeless for conducive learning, as there are far too many distractions. Obviously I am judging from personal experience; experts would probably say that *true academics* can thrive in any environment.

The only time I came close to excellence at school was on my second year physics exam when I came second to top with a 97%.

This was something of a miracle, as in previous terms my marks had been, on average, only 27% or 28%. Mum was convinced that she had a budding physicist on her hands, but I knew the truth.

We had a new teacher that year. His name was Mr. Bunker and I was absolutely terrified of him, so I went to great pains to complete all the homework he set and actually sit up and pay attention in his class. I never really understood much of his lessons but was far too shy to say so and just learnt everything parrot fashion.

Needless to say, the following year when he was no longer teaching us - apparently, due to an incident where he abandoned some girls at the swimming pool because they dallied too long drying their hair - I reverted to my usual position at the bottom of the class. I was never to regain ascendancy, much to Mum's distress.

French lessons often passed in a pleasant haze as we passed around a dog-eared copy of *The Passion Flower Hotel* wrapped in textbook brown paper. Every once in a while there would be a stifled giggle as one of us got to a sexy bit, then the boring old goody-goodies in the class would turn around and glare at us.

Some of the lessons I loved, such as English, art, and history, but I hated the traditional girls classes of needlework and domestic science. These always seemed to be run by middle-aged women who felt that unless a girl could become "homely," she was obviously not up to much. Remember that this was in the early 1960s; bras had yet to be burned and "good girls" definitely didn't have babies without being married. I was, in reality, quite good at sewing. Mum had been a tailor, sewing for smart establishments in London's Savile Row before I was born. I had learnt more from her than in all my sewing lessons at school, but I was written off by some of these teachers as having no ability at all. I was also pilloried for my attempts at cooking, though this was probably more justified. After all, how many people do you know who can manage to burn their cauliflower cheese during a mock O-Level exam?

Art lessons were always fun, both because of their content and our teacher. Mr. Lacey was a lovely man, introducing us to such delights as still life and self-portraits, although all we really wanted was to learn how to paint nudes.

There were two art rooms: the official one in the main school building and the other one, which was of the purpose-built, prefabricated huts at the end of the drive. In our final years we preferred the latter, as it gave you a spectacular view of the sixth form next door. These young men were a year our senior, so they were certainly considered to be well worth watching. My first proper boyfriend came from that class, so all those hours of illicit viewing were obviously worthwhile.

For some time, I had secretly nurtured a passion for Michael Vickers, an athletic, confident chap who seemed well out of my reach. At a Christmas party just before my 16th birthday, we danced and a spark was lit. As he walked me home, we talked about ourselves - trying to impress as you do - and I learnt that his grandfather had been Will

Hay, the comedian. I had never heard of him so this meant absolutely nothing to me, but Mum was quite impressed when I told her.

Mick and I were a couple for the next 18 months, utterly devoted. Or so I thought. I eventually discovered his outings with a girl called Pamela, whose father managed the local cinema and gave her free tickets. I was heartbroken. In my head I had already planned our future, down to the colours of the bridesmaid dresses at our wedding and how many babies we would have.

Seriously though, I grew up a lot during the bulk of our relationship and had a wonderful time. Had we not been so young I daresay it would have lasted a lot longer. Another thing that caused a real breach between us (Pamela aside) was when I decided not to continue in the sixth form to do my A-levels, but to leave school and make a career in banking.

University was never an option for me; no one in our family had ever achieved such a thing and I was too insecure about my abilities to imagine I was good enough for it. Mick was very ambitious and clever, and he felt that I was wasting myself. He intended to become a teacher and thought that I should do the same.

I stuck by my decision, however, and in October of 1967, I began my new career. Barclays Bank appointed me as a junior clerk, and on my first day I arrived at the North Sutton branch feeling very nervous. Within a few hours I was totally relaxed though, due to the warm welcome from my new colleagues. By the end of the week, I loved the job.

Together with the other two junior clerks, Janet and Brenda, I was responsible for filing away all the bank statements and cheques (quite a large and monotonous task no longer necessary these days due to computerisation) and then sending them out to customers as required. After several months of training, we also answered the telephone and dealt with simple requests. However, our *most important* task was to run over to the supermarket whenever any of our colleagues felt in need of a bar of chocolate or bag of crisps! Every day, we took it in turn to do the local clearing. This was quite an envious task except in the depths of winter, as it involved going to another bank in the High Street to meet up with other junior clerks from each of the big four banks (Barclays, National Provincial, Lloyds, and Martins) to exchange all the cheques. It was a terrific way of meeting new people, and on the way back to work we would have to stop and run errands for the rest of the staff: buy a licorice rock from the little sweetshop by the main post office, sticky buns from that special bakery at the top of the High Street, or get some cheese from British Home Stores.

My colleagues were extremely kind. Linda, Chris, and Maureen were all engaged to be married, and I loved to hear of their wedding plans and watch them ticking off the days on the big calendar behind their desks. There was Tina - just returned from her honeymoon, Mr. Lougher, Malcolm, Stuart - the very dishy young messenger, and the rather stern but kind branch manager who always sported a bow tie and ate his lunch at the Grapes public house on the corner opposite.

Saturday morning opening was standard then, and we took it in turn to be on duty. I really loved my Saturday shifts. Rules were relaxed and the men were allowed to wear sports jackets instead of their usual dark suits. We girls discarded our brown nylon Alexandre overalls - not quite as elegant as the smart uniforms Barclays staff wear today - and slipped into something more fashionable. Trousers were very much frowned upon for female staff unless it was bitterly cold, so we all wore our miniskirts. At that time, I was very much into my "false" phase, so on Saturday mornings I would often wear my false hairpiece, false eyelashes, and fake fingernails, the final always painted to match my outfit. I had thought the false eyelashes were an improvement to my look until a neighbour asked Mum if anything was wrong, as she had met me whilst out shopping and thought my eyes looked awfully sore!

After my six months of initial training at the bank I was to be transferred to another branch: Ewell Court, near Kingston in Surrey. I was terribly upset at having to leave my new friends, but they threw me a little farewell party and presented me with a huge card and a white lacy nightdress. Before I knew it, off I was for another adventure.

Within a short space of time, I had settled happily into the new branch and came to love the customers and staff alike. There was old Mr. Fancourt, who was the chief cashier, Gerry, Ann, Leanda, Roger, and Mrs. K., whose brand-new Mini was stolen from right outside the bank one day with only the door handles left as evidence!

My new role as a cashier was a delight, as it combined socialising with the excitement of tallying up the money correctly at the end of each day. Thanks to Leanda's tuition, I became extremely adept at counting banknotes and adding up huge columns of figures in my head. This was a very useful asset, as by now I was earning a small fortune for myself. My first month's salary was twenty eight pounds, so, working on an expected income for the year of nearly five hundred pounds, I began to make big plans.

Clothes were a must, but several trips to Chelsea Girl and Bus Stop soon sorted that out. My social life was becoming more varied and as I often begged Mum to "please run me up a dress by tomorrow evening," I took out a small loan and bought her an electric sewing machine. Sadly, I think she secretly hated it and still much preferred to sew by hand, at least until her arthritis made it impossible to do so.

The biggest part of my plan was to get myself mobile, so I enrolled with the British School of Motoring and nervously went for my first lesson. My instructor was a lovely lady called Mrs. Wiles, and after ten lessons and a hair-raising trip 'round Hyde Park Corner, I took my test. All went reasonably well except for reversing around a corner, but to my utter dismay I failed.

"Not to worry," said Mrs. Wiles, and she promptly booked me in for another test straight away. One month and one day later on a sunny July afternoon, I passed on my second attempt and began to look longingly at cars. Obviously, on my small salary it was going to be difficult to buy anything for a while, but Susan came to the rescue and lent me the enormous sum of eighty pounds. With it I bought a 1957 Morris Minor 1000, registration 779MMY, and it became my pride and joy. It was a little temperamental and often didn't start in the mornings, but generally it was well-behaved and we had such fun together. I installed a Wrigley's chewing gum machine on the dashboard, and my friends and I would put in our sixpences every time we fancied a chew. Having the car made social outings so much easier; no more long walks home after missing the last bus or hoping someone would have borrowed their parents' car. And oh what a joy when dancing with a boy who offered you a lift home, to be able to refuse gracefully by saying that you had your own transport. It also meant that Dad didn't have to spend so much time hanging around at cold bus stops, waiting for me to return from a jaunt.

I had so much fun in the two years after I left school - I loved my job and the independence it gave me.

With my friend Jen, I attended dances at church halls, parties, went ten pin bowling. I then graduated to Mondays, and sometimes Saturday evenings at the Orchid Ballroom in Purley. Here the boys seemed far more exciting, and it was so thrilling to spend ages in the girls powder room ensuring that when you finally emerged, your entrance into the throbbing and exciting atmosphere would be noticed. Sadly this was not always the case, as there were so many girls who were much older, prettier, and more sophisticated, but the excitement of the chase was there. Several big stars appeared there on the revolving stage under the huge, shiny disco ball, but not even the Small Faces or Georgie Fame and the Blue Flames could take away from the main attraction of our evenings: the boys. We very soon realised the importance of standing out in such a crowd, and to this end we visited Laurence Corner, a government surplus store where we purchased white sailor's trousers for 7s6d a pair. We wore these with white, frilly blouses and under the bright lights on the dance floor, we certainly seemed to get noticed. Someone later told us that these lights made white clothes appear transparent - oh well!

During this time of newfound freedom, I went on a few dates with some really nice boys. There was Stuart, a student at Oxford University, and David Songhurst, a very good-looking young man with a blue Mini and a beautiful voice. Both were older than me, quite sophisticated and very charming, but I was far too young to fully appreciate them. Despite wonderful evenings at the Castle pub in Richmond, the Putney Boathouse, and the spires of Oxford followed by Dr. Zhivago at the cinema, I foolishly let them both slip away.

Most Saturday afternoons would find a crowd of us at Wrights Coffee Bar in Epsom. To the frustration of the owners we would have just one cup of frothy coffee each, which we would dally over for an hour or so, supplemented occasionally by a plate of chips covered in tomato sauce. This was a very important ritual; not only was it a chance to meet up after a hard week's work, but it also gave us the opportunity to discuss the evening's plans. When it was made obvious that we had outstayed our welcome, we would sometimes go to visit Milky. His real name was Graham Way (the nickname given for obvious reasons), and on Saturdays he worked on the fruit and veg stall at the market. During the week I think he was a trainee architect or something.

Clothes:

Epsom Market was a great place to shop for dress materials and earrings.

Plastic clip-on earrings could be purchased really cheaply, and once painted with the coloured nail varnish of one's choice, they looked quite splendid. On one occasion I bought some incredibly cheap, shiny, flimsy red lining material which, to Mum's horror, I made into a dress. I wore it that very night to a dance at St. Ebba's church hall, together with my false hairpiece, false nails, eyelashes, and plastic earrings painted bright red to match. At that period of my life, poor Mum was often too embarrassed to be seen with me, as I paraded round in my minis, maxis, falsies, and jumble sale buys!

Sometimes on a Sunday, Jen and I would arrange to meet after church and if the weather was fine we would take a packed lunch and walk through the woods to Box Hill near Dorking. On arriving there, we might swim in the pool, or just wallow in the huge inner tubes they loaned out. These were great for me, as a non- swimmer, as I could recline gracefully in them and never admit to my ineptitude. Often this would be followed by a burger from the little restaurant opposite, then a quick wander round the hill to see if we knew anyone, followed by either a long walk home, or if we were really lucky, a life from a desirable male acquaintance. This was before the days of my little car of course, after that we were totally independent.

Another Sunday treat was to go to the local newsagent's in Tadworth to purchase a forbidden copy of the News of the World. This would be devoured from cover to cover before discussing at length the various scandals and dramas we had so enjoyed reading about.

Growing up:

In the early summer of 1968, when Jen and I were just 17, we persuaded our parents that we were responsible enough to take a holiday alone. As we only had small incomes, we decided that youth hostelling was the answer. We spent many happy hours poring over maps and planning our routes. To ensure we would have beds available, we sent off postal orders to cover our booking fees of seven shillings and sixpence per night and packed our rucksacks in anticipation. On the appointed day, we caught a train from Tadworth to Victoria Station, and from there we boarded a National coach to Hastings in East Sussex.

After disembarking we explored the seaside town, delighting in the castle, caves, pier, and rocky beach. Little did I imagine that one day some twenty or so years later, I would return to this place to live.

We were booked that night into the youth hostel at Guestling, some distance from the town, and after an exhausting day of walking, we stumbled into our beds in the girls dormitory.

The rest of the week was spent exploring East Sussex. We visited Alfriston and stayed two extra nights in the hostel there, though we were fined for getting back late - after 10.30pm - and punished with having to do our own washing up after breakfast as well as another pile. We did our own cooking on this holiday, and as the only meal I can recall is a corned beef hash with hard, raw carrots, I guess neither of us were skilled in the culinary stakes. After Alfriston we moved on to Brighton. We explored the little antique shops in the Lanes, walked on the pier, and settled on the beach with our sketch books. We were both keen on painting and we had decided that we were far more likely to attract boys if we appeared to be artists, rather than mere sun worshippers. This tactic seemed to work pretty well and we met two very interesting young men from Liverpool. With their long hair and gentle manners but rather scruffy appearances, we knew our mothers would have had a fit if they had seen us together.

One of them gave me a parting gift - a beautiful glass paperweight which he had found in a junk shop. This started my collection mania. Over the years since, I have amassed various collections; in my heyday, I owned about forty-five glass paperweights, fifty teapots, fourteen china and papier-mâché boxes, shells, pebbles, and rocks galore, and fledgling collections of ducks, cheese dishes, jugs, and small wooden items. Throughout the years I have managed to somewhat curb my magpie instincts, but they are always there, hovering at the back of my imagination and waiting to swoop in whenever an attractive article comes into sight.

After returning home at the end of the week, we decided that our trip had been most successful and should be repeated next year. As we appeared to have come to no harm (we didn't mention the underage drinking or long-haired young men), our parents reluctantly agreed to us taking a whole fortnight the next time.

When you are young and just starting out in life, things change very rapidly. By the time the next summer came 'round, we were both involved in new relationships.

Jen was dating Andrew, who was later to become her husband, and I was with Paul, a gentle, dark-haired apprentice, a master carpenter, of whom I was very fond. Mum rather disapproved of him because he had longish hair and was only a tradesman. Paul was one of the crowd who met at Wrights Coffee Bar on Saturdays, and we began dating after his broken engagement to a girl from the shoe shop (and my brief flings with a couple of Davids and a Charlie)!

One of our first dates was a fancy dress party. I went along as Hiawatha in one of Mum's old brown patterned curtains, cut down and fringed at the hem. With my long hair in plaits and wearing an authentic beaded headdress and fertility necklace that Jen's mum had lent me, I felt quite good, but was still wildly envious of Jen, who due to her good figure and wavy locks, was able to go as Mae West!

I had lots of fun with Paul. He was a year older than me and owned an Austin 1100 car and together with other friends from "the crowd" we went on day trips to places like Camber Sands. For one particular trip I borrowed a lilac towelling bikini, spent far too long in the sun - without sun cream, of course - and ended the day looking like a bright pink lobster. We went to the races, picnics, parties, dances, and pubs. By now I was eighteen and could drink legally; what a joy to be able to order a vodka and lime or sweet cider without fear of reprisal.

It was during my time with Paul that I learnt to drive. He was very encouraging, even to the extent of allowing me to practise once or twice in his precious car. When I eventually passed my test, dressed to kill in a navy and pale blue dress with a matching beaded handbag, I think he was as delighted as I was.

All was well on the romantic front and nothing could have possibly hinted at what was to be the momentous outcome of our second youth hostelling trip.

With two weeks at our disposal, we decided to venture farther afield. After some discussion, we agreed on South Devon.

Once more we mounted a National coach, complete with our huge rucksacks and paper knickers. These were a little experiment to save us doing too much washing whilst we were away. They turned out to be a great success until it rained, whereupon they fell to pieces!

We descended from the coach at Plymouth Bus Station, and after a little investigation of our whereabouts, we walked to our pre-booked hostel just outside the city centre.

Having ensured that we packed several flimsy little dresses in addition to the cord jeans and cheesecloth shirts we were wearing, we were well able to cope with the enjoyable, but rather limited socialising offered at the hostel. Our brand-new Levi jeans - shrunk for the occasion by spending a couple of hours wearing them in the bath - were also on hand in case the need arose to make a *really* good impression.

Our next port of call was Bigbury Bay. After an intense perusal of our maps, we realised that to walk there or rely on buses was not ideal, so despite promises to our parents, we decided to hitchhike. Reading this now, I wonder why we didn't take my car, but of course it was pretty ancient and not altogether reliable, so I guess we obviously decided not to risk it on such a long journey. We were very lucky; the whole fortnight passed in a flurry of excitement with no unpleasant incidents at all. Nothing on earth would induce me to hitch these days now that I am aware of all the dangers, but of course when you are young, you think you are bulletproof. We accepted rides in laundry vans where we had to curl up on top of sacks full of washing, another in an egg farmer's truck where we were terrified that all the eggs would smash as we hurled 'round the narrow country lanes. Then there was the sales rep, his car jammed full of leather samples and suitcases. Our favourite, however, was the beaten up, psychedelically-painted van belonging to a wannabe rock group.

We stayed at super hostels at Bigbury, Salcombe, Maypool, and Lownard. We saw lots of the countryside, with side trips to Dartmouth, Totnes, and Kingsbridge. Then it was time to return to Plymouth, where we indulged in a little last minute shopping. I bought a pretty but rather transparent petticoat, which I was convinced I could wear as a dress, and some expensive French aftershave to take home as a present for Paul. Sadly, we boarded the homeward bound coach and the first part of our journey was fairly uneventful. We stopped at Exeter, and after leaving our rucksacks on the back seat to bag our places, we entered the cafeteria.

Little did I know that the events of the next ten minutes were to change the course of my entire life.

The cafeteria at Exeter Bus Station was much the same as such establishments anywhere in the world. We settled down to enjoy our rubbery cheese sandwiches and mediocre coffee. Two young men came to sit opposite, and smilingly asked to borrow our salt and pepper despite the fact that their table was already laden down with cruet sets. As we made our way back to the coach, we bemoaned the lack of such decent chaps amongst our fellow passengers. Imagine our delight then to find the aforesaid gentlemen sitting on our coach, just two rows ahead of us. Apparently, they had travelled from Newquay and had been forced to change coaches for the final part of their journey. Spotting our rucksacks and having no desire to sit with a couple of hippies, they had instead chosen a forward seat.

A little bribery in the form of Cornish Clotted Cream toffees soon secured a swap of seats and the two men joined us in the back row. We spent the remainder of the journey exchanging holiday stories and trying to impress each other, and by the time *he* left the coach at Aldershot, I was besotted.

His name was Richard, and he was a tall, dark, handsome salesman.

Smitten as I now was with Richard, I thought there was no room in my life for other men. Sadly, Paul and I parted. Actually - that is not strictly true. I am very ashamed to say that I just dumped him on my doorstep that very evening, although I did give him the French aftershave. That is one of the things I regret in my life; he was a good person who did not deserve to be treated so shabbily. Perhaps one day I will get the chance to apologise to him. I understand he now lives in Australia, so perhaps I should just track him down and cross the Tasman.

Soon after, I began a schedule of fortnightly trips down to Aldershot in my little car. Richard didn't drive, so he would come up on the train one week and I would go down to him the next. As we only saw each other once a week, things were blissful. It is terribly easy to be on your best behaviour for such a short time.

Within a few months, I was proudly wearing a tiny diamond engagement ring and looking forward to a life of joy and content- ment with my lovely husband, beautiful home, and the two or more children we planned to have.

At the tender age of nineteen, I thought I knew everything. Despite Mum's disapproval and Dad's very grave reservations, I went ahead and booked and paid for my beautiful white wedding. I was going to have six bridesmaids, a reception at the Red Coach rooms at Nork, and a Paris honeymoon.

In the car on the way to the church, wearing the beautiful, white, satin wedding dress I had designed for myself, Dad suddenly leant over and touched me gently on the arm.

"We don't have to do this, love; we can always ask the driver to turn the car 'round and go home." My dad, a man who rarely expressed his opinion, was obviously very unsure that I was making the right decision.

But of course I knew best, and having overcome a few problems with Richard's family, who were strict Irish Catholics and rather against him taking a Protestant wife, we were finally married on a cold spring day just two weeks after my twentieth birthday. We married at the Parish Church of St. Mary the Virgin at Burgh Heath.

MARRIAGE

The first few years passed very quickly as I settled into my new life as wife, career girl, and homemaker.

Without realising it, I had led a rather sheltered life in the bosom of my family and I was ill-prepared for the reality of life with a full-time job, a home to clean and organise, and a rather demanding new husband, who needed feeding, washing, and ironing.

Optimism again to the fore, I vowed to become the perfect partner. Gradually, I learnt the best ways to cook without ruining everything, clean 'til the place shone, and sew curtains and cushions (all by hand, as I had no machine). For the first couple of years, I didn't even have a washing machine, so I used to trample the bed linen in the bath to get it clean. It was not until later that I realised it was much easier to just pop down the road to the launderette.

I discovered a real joy in home making which was just as well, as by the time we had been married for two years, we were moving house for the third time.

At first, we lived in a flat in Farnham in Surrey, and I drove to work at Barclays Bank in Aldershot every day. I had hoped for a transfer to the Farnham branch so that I could walk to work, but there was no vacancy. Aldershot was fun though; it was quite a change from provincial Surrey and I enjoyed the work and my new colleagues.

Owned by Richard's employers, Courts Furnishers, our new home was the bottom half of an old Victorian house with beautifully proportioned rooms. Here began my passionate interest in interior design.

It was agreed that if we decorated the house ourselves, the company would pay for all the materials. I chose beautiful Sanderson wallpapers - orange and green paisley for the lounge and dining room - matched with orange painted Windsor chairs. My godmother had given me these chairs and I lovingly restored and painted them to suit the current fashion. I chose orange and lemon patterned wallpaper for the kitchen and larder, and all my old glass coffee jars were given orange labels to match. There was a little sun room leading off from our bedroom and here I planned to have my easel and paints to escape to on sunny evenings and produce a few masterpieces. Sadly this dream was never fulfilled, as the first time I ventured into that room, the floor gave way and collapsed due to dry rot.

Despite its need for improvements, I loved my first little home and was absolutely heartbroken when after just four months, Richard's company asked him to transfer to the Richmond on Thames branch. It was a promotion for him, so sadly I choked back my tears and asked for yet another transfer in the bank, then packed my suitcase. Although Richard's new branch was only about thirty miles away, the company preferred their managers and assistant managers live near to the stores so that they were always available in case of emergencies, faulty alarms, or break- ins. Our new flat at Kingston Hill was also owned by the company, and was this time the top half of a large Victorian house. After a while I came to love the lofty rooms, despite the fact that they were absolutely freezing and the only heating we had was a one-bar electric fire in the sitting room. Decorating was rather more frugal here as we had to pay for it ourselves, so my artistic talent had to content itself with turquoise and orange walls, orange vision net curtains, turquoise blue drapes, and a turquoise carpet. The carpet - the biggest we could afford - was not sufficient to cover the enormous room, so to make up for the deficit I painted the remaining floorboards bright orange.

Despite my initial reservations, I thoroughly enjoyed my eighteen-month stay in Kingston. I worked at the very busy branch of Barclays bank in Clarence Street - opposite Bentalls department store - and lunchtimes were spent wandering around the shops with my newfound friends. Sometimes, on the occasional sunny day, we would eat our sandwiches in the churchyard or take a stroll along the River Thames and stop at the Rowbarge public house to partake in a refreshing glass of cider and some of their delicious prawn sandwiches. The above choice depended on our state of impecuniosity. If it was the end of the month and payday, we could afford the pub.

This was the most cosmopolitan place in which I had worked so far and I just loved the diversity of customers. Some days, the people I encountered would include not only the expected smattering of housewives with pretty babies to admire, rich business men, shopkeepers, and pub landlords all queuing to deposit their vast sums, but also exotic and charming foreign visitors and instantly recognisable actors and rock stars. I can assure you that it is extremely difficult to keep up a totally professional image when issuing ten pound notes to the film star of your dreams.

I became extremely fond of some of my colleagues. There was Kay - the head cashier, who became like an extra mum to me, Roger, Jane, John, Pauline, Eileen, and Pam - my fellow cashiers. When Pauline was pregnant and suffering from morning sickness, we took it in turns to make cheese and crackers for her to eat before the bank opened at 9.30 so that she wouldn't greet the customers looking too green!

Staff Christmas parties were always great fun here. Because it was such a big branch there was always someone new to talk to, and of course everyone let their hair down so you could see them in quite a new light. The first year I wore my home-crocheted mini dress; it was kingfisher blue and quite tiny. The holes were so large that for decency's sake, I had been forced to dye a bra, knickers, and slip to wear underneath. The following year, being older and wiser, I opted for a more decorous look and wore my silver lurex, full-length, backless number!

I was very sad when the time came to leave Kingston, but the sadness was tinged with excitement as we were going to become homeowners for the first time.

Richard's company had offered him another promotion, this time to Ely in Cambridgeshire. As property was much cheaper there, we decided that we could just about afford to buy a house of our own.

After several reconnaissance trips, we found just what we were looking for - an almost new, three bedroom, semi-detached house on a small estate on the outskirts of the town for just £8750. Even before contracts were exchanged, I had mentally planned the complete interior, right down to the orange and yellow tea towels for the kitchen.

It took longer than planned for the sale to be completed due to the vendors - a charming but rather scatty Irish lecturer and his sweet but quiet wife. They seemed to live quite chaotically, with mountains of books all over the house and five children all under the age of three.

This delay meant that our first four months in Ely were spent in the home of a charming couple, Mr. and Mrs. Grey. Their lovely old Georgian town house was full of antiques and collectables, many of them having been found at local country house sales and auctions. I loved to sit in the warmth of their kitchen whilst Mrs. Grey baked bread on her AGA and her husband reminisced about his years as a pig farmer in the Cambridgeshire Fens. The Greys were extremely kind to me, so welcoming and generous, and being with them made up a little for being so far away from my own family for the first time in my life.

As I had a few days holiday before starting work, I was able to spend many happy hours wandering the old cathedral city, quickly becoming familiar with not only the fine architecture in Cathedral Close, but also all the interesting little shops that lined Fore Street. I loved the slow country atmosphere and the fact that people had time to stop and chat. Quite a contrast to bustling old Kingston. On sunny days, I took my old Austin Cambridge on trips to the outlying Fen villages or went for gentle strolls along the banks of the River Ouse.

I never had quite the same fondness for any car after my old Morris 1000 finally bit the dust. Sadly, she had a very undignified ending at the local scrapyard, due to her sagging bottom which needed more welding than I could afford.

Thursdays in Ely were a particular delight, for that was market day. Although the wares for sale were decidedly twentieth century, there was still a faintly medieval atmosphere about the whole proceedings. Folk would come in from all the surrounding villages; for many, it was their only outing of the week. To see them stepping off the buses with their empty wicker baskets and talk of sugar beet prices, I found it easy to imagine the same scene one hundred years earlier with farm carts and bonnets replacing the buses and headscarves. It was the one day that the city really came alive and the streets were packed with happy, gossiping crowds intent on spending their hard-earned cash. The fish and chip shop stayed open all day, as seemingly did the Market Square public houses, and it was impossible to get a seat at the matinee show at the old Rex Cinema.

There was one particular stall that was always very popular; it sold dress materials: lace, buttons, ribbons, and zips, all at amazingly cheap prices. I once bought a whole roll of pink ribbon for just twenty-five pence. I knew it was a bargain, but never for one moment imagined that despite using it to make ribbon baby dresses, decorating gifts and cakes galore, giving yards to friends for their sewing projects, and even using it on occasion in place of garden twine, it would still be around to haunt me some twenty years later. I swear that it must have been at least a hundred miles long! Ely Market Place was often the setting for the unusual and quirky;

I remember on one occasion watching Clement Freud (hopeful Member of Parliament and relative of the more famous Sigmund) showing off his culinary skills by preparing tasty tidbits for passing shoppers.

I set off with some trepidation for my first day at work. You would imagine that having had to change branches so many times I would be nonchalant by now, but I still got butterflies thinking about it. Unfortunately, there had not been a vacancy at the Ely branch of Barclays, so I was transferred instead to Soham, a little village some 10 miles away.

Here, I was delighted to find a tiny and very close-knit community. There were just eight members of staff and apart from the manager, his assistant Graham, and the head cashier, who was a charming ex RAF officer, they were all local girls: Sue, Sheila, Barbara, and Kathy, born and bred in the village with generations of ancestors buried in the churchyard.

I quickly made friends and life settled into a pleasant pattern. The work was very enjoyable and I soon learnt from the customers a little about pig farming and harvesting sugar beet. On the way home, I would often stop at little roadside cottages to buy strawberries, eggs, tomatoes, or beautiful fresh-cut flowers, and the owners would be happy to stop and chat with me. I loved their gentle country accents. Occasionally I made a bad mistake and got carried away, like the time I bought an enormous 50lb sack of carrots. I then spent a whole evening peeling, washing, and blanching them, readying them for the freezer.

By now, we were installed in the new house, duly decorated and furnished to my mental plan. Amongst other little luxuries, we had purchased the freezer, and because of my desire to mother at least half a dozen infants, I had chosen the largest one I could find. To fill it, I baked my own bread and froze as many fruits and vegetables as I could lay my hands on.

I became very broody during this time; I was in my early twenties and very idealistic. My family members were miles away, so I only saw them a few times a year. Although I had friends and a job I enjoyed, I was a little lonely and longed for babies of my own for which I could love and care.

Richard's career was going very well but financially things were still tight, so when he suggested waiting for another six months or so to have children, I reluctantly agreed. In my usual impulsive manner, I then rushed out and spent a few pounds on beautiful baby clothes and linens in anticipation of the great event, and placed them carefully in a drawer, wrapped in lavender-scented tissue.

I loved that house in Ely, until the mouse invasion.

Since I was quite tiny I had been absolutely terrified of mice, despite the fact that my favourite cartoon character was Mickey Mouse and, apart from the occasional brief sighting in the children's corner at Chessington Zoo, I had managed to steer quite clear of them.

One weekend, my mum and youngest sister, Margaret, came to stay and we decided to go into town shopping. It was a very successful trip and amongst other things, I found a delightful pair of shoes reduced to half price in the Co-Op. They were quite beautiful - navy blue soft leather courts with emerald green toes and heels. Of course, I just had to have them. After our pleasant and rewarding afternoon we were very thirsty when we got home, so I went straight to the kitchen to put the kettle on. Mum suddenly shrieked, having seen a little mouse run across the floor. Although I hadn't seen it myself, I screamed loudly and jumped onto the nearest chair. Of course, all that sudden movement frightened the little creature and he apparently scooted away before Mum could trace his whereabouts.

Despite Mum's efforts to calm us, Margaret, aged ten, and I were not convinced he was truly gone. I insisted that we shut ourselves in the upstairs bathroom with all the plugs installed in the sinks and bath until the invader was found. Several hours later with no further sightings, and life resumed to normal. By the time our visitors left the next day, having not actually seen the mouse myself, I was quite complacent and convinced that Mum had merely imagined the scene.

This was not the case. When the rodent reappeared a week later, I was nearly hysterical. Richard was no help, as he too was a bit scared of the furry little creature. The girls at work thought my fears were extremely peculiar; they had grown up on the Fens and told me that now, because I lived in the country, I must get used to such things. Having decided that I would rather die than share my home with such unwelcome visitors, I rang the local council and asked the rodent man to call.

On the appointed day I rushed home from work, fully expecting to see a formidable character in wellies, toting a shotgun. I was rather disappointed to find an elderly gentleman in a navy blue suit holding a clipboard. However, he was very polite and pleasant, and although obviously quietly amused, was very sympathetic to my problem. He explained that because our house was surrounded by sugar beet fields, the mouse likely came in from there. Although he usually dealt with farmers overrun with rats or other vermin, because I was obviously terrified, he felt sure he could help me too!

Good as his word, he discovered that they were coming in through a tiny gap in the garage wall. With his help, just two weeks and fourteen mice later, I was cured.

Shortly after this episode, Richard decided another move was necessary. He was very ambitious and felt he would progress faster back in the South East of England, so very sadly I said goodbye to my new friends, sold the house, packed up yet again and prepared to move to Aldershot in Hampshire.

Aldershot. The very name conjures up a picture of a rather seedy garrison town, and I would be lying if I pretended the reality was any different in the early 1970s. After just a few months living there, however, I found myself fiercely defending the town's reputation if anyone was critical. In truth, it was certainly not somewhere I would have chosen to live, but having no option, I was determined to make the best of it.

For the first few months, we had to live with Richard's mother and stepfather in Ash Vale until our new house was ready for occupation.

We had bought a brand-new, three bedroom end-of-terrace house on a small estate. It wasn't as nice as the home I left behind in Ely, but in no time at all I had decorated it in subtle shades of beige and brown, the orange floorboards being a thing of my feckless youth, made curtains and cushions galore, and put labels on all the glass storage jars in the tiny kitchen.

The garden was exactly as the builders had left it, with bricks, rubble, and steel girders fighting for space among the ten-foot high weeds.

Because it was a new challenge, I decided to become a gardener. Within a few years the space was completely transformed with patios, beautiful shrubs and flowers, and a fence that blew down every winter, wrecking my climbing roses!

Life soon settled into a familiar pattern.

I hadn't been able to get a transfer back to the branch in Aldershot where I started my married life, so I was now working at Barclays in Camberley High Street instead. For the first week or two I found the pace exhausting compared to the easy working life I had in Soham. Very soon, I had established rapport with my new colleagues and went on to form several lasting friendships. With David and Valerie, we went regularly to West End theatres or simply spent happy days with their three small sons. With Sue and Dave, we enjoyed such delights as medieval banquets and the Eton Wine Bar.

Having moved around the country at such a fast rate, our friends were scattered, but we often got together on weekends. Sometimes Jen and Andrew would come down from Norfolk, Dennis and Su from Gosport, and Buzz and June from Aylesbury, and despite my inauspicious beginnings in the kitchen (potatoes resembling bullets and soggy meringues), I eventually became a reasonable cook and loved to entertain.

Despite a fairly full social life I was still longing to have children, but was again persuaded by Richard to wait "just a little longer." Because I knew I still had many childbearing years left and desperately wanted my marriage to work, I choked back my disappointment and soldiered on. It was awfully hard, however, being brave when all my friends were showing off their beautiful babies.

I had learnt to ignore the darker side of my marriage.

Being wed so young, I had been quite unprepared for the reality of living with a man. Although we had lots of fun together, I was too gentle and soft-hearted to cope easily with his violent outbursts of temper and my discovering of his casual and extremely hurtful infidelities.

Still, as far as I was concerned, this marriage was for life and something always seemed to turn up to improve things: a promotion in my job, a summer holiday in Italy, Tunisia, Devon, or Greece, a new tumble dryer or Kenwood Food Chef; the list was endless!

After five years of marriage, something very special turned up.

Richard came home from work one evening, looking rather sheepish. Instantly I knew we were on the move again. With a heavy heart but trying desperately to look keen, I enquired as to our new home. Was it to be the West Country, the Midlands, or the Medway towns? To my amazement, he said, "No, they want us to go to Fiji."

Geography has never been my strong point, so I was convinced this was in the West Indies and began to get really excited. To be sure, we got out the atlas - this was way before the internet made research easy - and after studying it at some length, we were astonished to find the Fiji Islands, no more than a tiny pin prick, in the middle of the South Pacific Ocean. My adventurous spirit was now really aroused and I could hardly wait to begin this great journey. Much to my surprise though, Richard was a little reticent. He had felt quite settled and happy being back in his hometown, close to people and places he knew. He was not at all sure about embarking on such an adventure. Determined not to let the opportunity slip through our hands, I gently persuaded him that all would be well. After all, it was an excellent move career-wise and financially, and would certainly broaden our horizons.

It took several months for all the red tape to be dealt with. There were medicals, injections, and work permits from the government of Fiji, together with in-depth interviews with the company's board of directors to ensure that we could cope with the heat, cockroaches, and expatriate lifestyle.

Finally our fond farewells were said, along with the invitation that if anyone happened to be passing through (unlikely at 11,000 miles distant), they must drop in to say hello.

On the 24th September 1976, we finally set off with just four suitcases to last us the duration of our two-year stay.

My family could not believe that I, who always travelled with exceedingly heavy bags, could possibly cope with such a modest selection of luggage, but thanks to yards of swiss voile and fine cotton lawn fabrics, I had run up numerous little dresses suitable for my new life.

NEW ADVENTURES

The journey in and of itself was an adventure.

We flew from London Heathrow to Los Angeles with British Airways. After drinking cocktails in the airport lounge with a real-life Texan cowboy, we then boarded an Air New Zealand plane. After touching down briefly for refuelling in Honolulu, the rest of the flight was fairly uneventful, apart from the luxury of hot towels every time we woke and superb giant prawns for dinner. They were so delicious and succulent I could have eaten dozens.

Finally, after our lengthy travels, we landed at Nadi International Airport.

I had been dreaming of this moment for so many months and I was not the least bit disappointed.

As I stepped from the aircraft onto the tarmac, I was enveloped in the wonderfully warm, exotically-scented atmosphere that was soon to become so familiar. At five o'clock in the morning after leaving behind a cold and wet English autumn, it seemed exactly like heaven.

Nothing had prepared me for the sheer attractiveness of the native Fijians.

There were many handsome, smiling men in smart white shirts and sulus (wrap-around skirts) which showed off their dark, muscular legs. Beautiful girls shyly placed leis (flower garlands) around our necks and bade us welcome to their islands.

I was so enthralled watching these graceful people that I hardly noticed how long our baggage was taking to arrive on the carousel. I gradually became aware that our fellow passengers had all departed through customs. To add to our woes, my feet had swollen to at least quadruple their normal size due to the long flight, and the numerous mosquitoes there were absolutely thrilled to discover fresh blood. Unperturbed, we made discreet enquiries as to the whereabouts of our cases and after another half-hour wait, we were advised that unfortunately, they had probably gone to Hong Kong.

A little daunted by this news, along with the fact that I was now covered in dozens of mosquito bites, we dejectedly made our way through customs to be greeted by Richard's new boss and his wife. They took the situation into their own hands immediately and marched off to the airline desk demanding cash to replace some of our missing belongings. Bearing in mind we had mislaid absolutely everything, the twenty pounds we were given was barely enough to buy a few essentials. Therefore, my first two days in Fiji saw me wearing borrowed clothes and a bikini that was about three sizes too big!

I am happy to report that the aforesaid suitcases eventually reappeared three days later, having been to Hong Kong, Singapore, and New Zealand.

It was decided that because of possible jet lag, we should stay in a hotel near the airport for the first few days. This was a wonderful introduction to the luxurious lifestyle the islands offer to rich tourists, but I was longing to establish my own base and get to know the reality of my new home and its people.

On the third day, we considered ourselves sufficiently rested to begin real life and were driven to our new home. Fiji consists of several hundred islands, many of them uninhabited. Our new home was to be on Viti Levu in Lautoka. Lautoka, known as the Sugar

City, is the second largest city on Fiji's main island, the largest being the capital, Suva. In the 1970s, Lautoka had a population of some 12,000 people. It is situated about 20 miles north of the airport and the drive from it is a pleasant one past local villages - both Fijian and Indian - and large sugarcane plantations. By the time we reached Lautoka Wharf, I could hardly contain my excitement. Just think, I had a whole two years to explore this fascinating place; I could barely wait to get started.

As the car turned into our new driveway I blinked hard so that no-one would see my welling tears. Could it possibly be true that I, who had grown up in a comfortable but modest council house, was to live in such splendour?

Amidst beautiful gardens full of colourful hibiscus, perfumed frangipani flowers, and banana and coconut trees, stood my new home. It was large and imposing, built in the typical local style in what was quaintly, but accurately known as a "concrete house."

In a quiet cul-de-sac of just half a dozen similar properties, it was light and airy, with large windows and French doors leading onto large balconies. Built on two levels, it was cleverly designed to make the most of its wonderful setting by having large windows on two sides of each room. The sitting, dining, and balcony areas overlooked the front, whilst the bedrooms and bathrooms were on the lower level at the back of the house. Underneath was an enormous carport, a laundry room, and a separate flat.

Not only was I to live in such splendour, I was also going to be spoilt outrageously, as local colonial tradition apparently decreed that it was impossible for a white woman to look after her own home in such a hot climate. I was persuaded - much against my better judgement, for I had no desire to encourage the class system - to employ a house-girl.

Naomi lived in the flat underneath the house and had been employed by the previous tenants, so was there to greet us on our arrival. Instantly I knew I had found a friend.

Within a day or two I was settled. It doesn't take very long to unpack four suitcases, and while Richard was busy with his new job, I set about learning all I could to help me understand my new home.

Fiji is a multi-racial society made up mainly of indigenous Fijians, Indians, Chinese, Europeans, Tongans, and other Polynesians. Many of the Indian population are descendants of the original indentured workers, sent by the old colonial government to labour in the sugar cane fields.

When I arrived there in 1976, the country had been independent for just six years and was still very proud to be not just part of the British Commonwealth, but also the 127th member of the United Nations. In many Fijian homes, a picture still hung of Queen Elizabeth II, whom they referred to as "our Queen."

History and economics had together created a country in which Fijians and Indians now co-existed in almost equal numbers. A potentially explosive situation, smouldering quietly in the late 1970s only to erupt violently in late 1987, then again in 2000 and 2006. Since then the country has settled down, and although there will always be political discord as there is in almost every country in the world, the Fijian society is pretty harmonious, with people from every background rubbing along together quite happily.

As an expat wife, I was not granted a work permit, so I had all the time in the world at my disposal. I soon realised how easy it was to be swept up into the true colonial lifestyle, with long, hot days spent lounging by the pool at the Northern Club, punctuated by coffee mornings, bridge parties, and golf. Having no desire to waste my precious two years in that way, I sought alternatives.

My initial feelings about Naomi had proved to be accurate, and within a couple of days I felt as though we had been friends forever.

She was a 33-year-old attractive Fijian woman with dark skin, beautiful, curly black hair, and the most wonderful smile. As she lived alone in the flat downstairs, I had assumed she was unmarried. To my surprise, I learnt that she had a husband and two small sons who lived in Soso village on her home island of Naviti, in the Yasawas. Probing gently, I enquired as to the reason for her family's separation and was amazed to hear that her previous European employers had not allowed her family to stay with her in the flat. Immediately, I said that they would always be welcome, as indeed would any of her extended family. It had not taken me long to realise that Fijians consider anyone from their home village to be a relative.

The very next week, my new family grew from just one to four.

Semesa, Naomi's quiet and gentle husband, and her two sons, Josevata (Jo) and Malelili (Ma), arrived on a small boat from Naviti. Within a very short space of time our family also included Dingo, a dog of very uncertain origins, and Marmalade, a tiny ginger kitten born under the house next door.

As the mistress of such a grand establishment, I had to learn to shop and housekeep to my best advantage; this proved to be a little more hair-raising than my once-routine weekly trip to Sainsburys. It sounds strange to write it now because the world has moved on so quickly since those days; nowadays there are many good supermarkets in Fiji, stocked with everything imaginable, and almost everyone walks around them clutching their mobile phones. Back in the 1970s, however, it was very different.

Although Lautoka was the second-largest city in Fiji, it was certainly not in any way comparable with cities or even large towns I had experienced to date.

It boasted two department stores, Morris Hedstrom and Burns Philp, and these stocked a small range of foodstuffs in addition to clothing, linens, tools, and electrical and garden equipment. My heart sank as I wheeled my trolley around the aisles; the food hall was roughly the size of a small English corner shop, but nothing like as well stocked. Most of the labels seemed quite alien to me;

no comforting tins of Heinz Baked Beans or packets of PG Tips here! Gradually I became used to Punjas tea, ghee (refined butter used in cooking), and Walu, a local fish not unlike cod. Handling the difference in milk was more of a problem for me as there was no fresh cow's milk available, although a little Indian man did walk the streets selling goat milk. Having tried both this and the sterilised bottle stuff, I opted for the safer, but more expensive tins of Australian evaporated milk. Watered down, this made quite an acceptable addition to tea and coffee, although it was a little hard on the waistline.

Obviously, there were an awful lot of items completely unavailable and I very quickly learnt to cope without them. Dry goods, such as rice and flour, came in enormous quantities, served in clear plastic bags. As long as you remembered to freeze them immediately, it was easy enough to sieve out the weevils.

Initially, I did not find it so easy to cope with the meat situation. The shops carried a small quantity of fresh meat and fish, but I was advised to buy the bulk of my meat down by the wharf, at Fiji Meats. At first sight it looked nothing like any butchers I had ever seen, for there was no meat on display at all. The smell was pretty overpowering to my delicate nostrils, and for a few minutes I seriously considered becoming a vegetarian. But the meat, once purchased, proved to be surprisingly good; the guys who worked there were lovely. In time, I learnt to telephone my order a day ahead, thereby allowing myself only a short time in the rather oppressive atmosphere.

The local market became one of my favourite places. While at first I was overwhelmed by the piles of exotic and brightly coloured fruits and vegetables on offer - *What on earth did one do with dalo and cassava?* - I soon realised that it was much better to go marketing early in the morning, before the sun was too high and the smells followed suit. Gradually, with the help of Naomi and my Marguerite Patten cookbook, I became confident enough to buy pawpaws, breadfruit, zucchinis, mangos, limes, and fresh coconut, and I delighted in getting to know the stallholders. I usually went to the market two or three times a week, and often spent at least half an hour wandering 'round, comparing prices and quality before buying. As well as the permanent stalls, the market was often packed with casual sellers, mostly village folk who had come into town especially to sell their excess produce. Side by side, Fijians and Indians squatted on the pavement, presiding over heaps of tomatoes, huge, green lemons, bananas, and pineapples. Watching them laughing, gossiping, and sitting under large umbrellas to shield themselves from the hot and relentless sun, it was easy to forget that for many families this was their only source of income and that the pitiful amounts raised in one day would scarcely buy a couple of cinema tickets back in England.

Conscious of this, I often found myself buying far more than I really needed. A heap of bananas from one person for twenty cents followed by another heap for twenty five cents from someone else, just because I wanted to help the families selling them. I soon became very adept at baking banana loaves, banana muffins, and banana cheesecake. Pineapples were another joy, once I had learnt from Naomi the best way to peel and cut them. They were usually sold in heaps of three or four very cheaply, together with watermelon, which was also ridiculously inexpensive to my Western eye. I often ate them for breakfast, lunch, and dinner.

Because it was such a small and friendly community, it was very easy to become involved. Within a short space of time, I was drafted onto various committees.

One of these was attached to the Red Cross, and we were responsible for producing a fortnightly newsletter to raise funds. Our committee consisted of six ladies who met once a month to discuss forthcoming issues. Because the Red Cross hall doubled up as a church and nursery school and was often unavailable, we would take it in turns to host the meetings in our own homes, of course having to provide coffee and cake to stimulate our journalistic minds.

The evening before the first committee meeting I was to attend, the retiring secretary (my neighbour Lois, a Kiwi girl whose position

I was to fill) phoned me to remind me to "take a plate." Being new to Fiji and rather naïve, I thought it was a pity that the hostess did not have enough china to cope and made a mental note to ensure I was not in such an embarrassing position when my turn came round. I put aside one of my best non-chipped plates and went to bed with a clear conscience.

Unbeknownst to me, it was a tradition in this part of the world to always take a contribution of food to a tea party. This was known as "taking a plate."

Imagine then, the horror on Lois's face when she arrived to collect me the next morning and spotted my empty plate.

"But Pat," she said, "where's your cake?"

After due explanation and much hysterical laughter, we went to the meeting via her house, where she gave me a delicious chocolate cake to pass off as my own. I didn't really enjoy that meeting very much, as I kept thinking of the awful humiliation I had barely escaped, but I accepted the offered position as committee secretary for News and Views and thereupon began a very happy two-year stint.

Finding enough editorial content for the newsletters was always a great problem, for very little of consequence happened at that time in Fiji and we were virtually untouched by the outside world. There was no television and certainly no internet at that time, so most of our little paper was filled with items of local interest, such as how many tons of sugar cane had been harvested, when the next hurricane was due, and how to marinate raw fish in coconut milk. We also reported on all the comings and goings of the expat and local community - who was getting married, having babies, passing exams, gaining promotion, or going home on leave. It was almost a tropical court circular!

The committee itself was a mini-United Nations.

The editor and driving force was a tiny and charming New Zealander, Margaret Stewart, wife of the local judge of the Supreme Court. She had lived in Fiji for many years, and apart from brief forays to visit her Kiwi offspring, was quite devoted to the island.

Under her guidance we worked very happily, although I never envied whoever got stuck with the job of visiting local businesses and trying to sell them advertising space.

Because we had such strict deadlines and were often short of helpers, it was not unusual to find yourself proofreading on Tuesdays, running off copies on the old Gestetner machine on Wednesdays, and compiling the paper on Thursdays.

In addition to being the secretary, I was part of the regular compiling team on Thursday afternoons. For two or three hours we would rush around with staples and glue, but there was always time to chatter while we worked. Our conversations were fascinating for we were a real mixed bunch of ladies. There were usually six or seven of us of Fijian, Indian, Tongan, Chinese, New Zealand, and Rhodesian (later known as Zimbabwe) origin. I formed the British contingent.

For two years we met and enjoyed each other's company, and in addition to the one thousand or so dollars we were able to contribute annually to Red Cross funds, we gained tremendous insight into our various cultures. I even tried, unsuccessfully, to learn a smattering of Fijian and Hindustani. At the end of our Thursdays, we would drag the heavy sacks of newsletters to my car. After dropping Mrs. Naidu home (her husband would not allow her to walk the streets unchaperoned), I would drive to the post office where the headman, a distant relative of Naomi's, would delight in telling me all the latest news and gossip. I came to know all the post room boys quite well, and would often stop for a chat when I went to collect my private mail every day. There was no such thing as letterboxes or postmen in Fiji then; all mail was addressed care of box numbers and had to be picked up from the main office in Vitogo Parade.

Aside from my time with the Red Cross committee, I also became a member of the Intellectually Handicapped Children's School committee. This was run entirely on voluntary contributions, and they had raised enough over the years to build a little school, complete with a playground and enough land for expansion. There were about 30 pupils in total, ranging in age from five to thirty years. Despite the quite severe handicaps of some of the pupils, the school was an extremely happy place for them. Under the devoted care of the principal, Master Nand, and his two assistant teachers, the pupils learnt many basic skills and formed caring friendships with each other.

On one memorable occasion, we enlisted students from the local high school to help us collect at a flag day, and the whole city was swarmed with eager sixteen year olds soliciting money from everyone that passed by.

Apart from being an extra pair of hands at fundraising events, my contribution to this very worthwhile charity was rather limited. However, I loved the pupils, and would occasionally bake some cakes to bring to them on a visit at breaktime. This was more a treat for me than them I suspect, as they were always delighted to see visitors and treated me like royalty.

On less busy days, I would occasionally take a trip with Lois to Field 40. In those days, this was a small Indian settlement just a few miles from the city centre. Many of the families who lived there were rather poor with bad living conditions.

Lois was a member of the YWCA, and as part of their field work, they would go to outlying villages such as this to teach basic skills like knitting and crocheting.

After just a few weeks, most of the ladies there had become much more accomplished at these handicrafts than either Lois or I, so our visits became merely social. We would be invited into several homes during each of our afternoons to drink gallons of very sweet tea and eat huge buttered biscuits.

Attractive, wide-eyed children would hang around, staring at us until they were chased away by their embarrassed mothers. Believe me when I say that it is awfully hard to avoid eating an unwanted fourth biscuit or drink another cup of that unbearably sweet milky tea when tiny eyes are piercing into your soul.

Determined not to miss any opportunities, I too had my fair share of learning new skills. I joined a craft class where we all pooled our resources; here I learnt patchwork, macrame, batik, and silk-screen printing. From then on, my house was filled with macrame hanging baskets and after I taught Naomi and her sister Nasau the skill - so was much of our neighbourhood.

The patchwork skills came in jolly useful at Christmas, when I made tea cosies for everyone in sight. As soon as I heard of another baby on the way to friends or family in England, I despatched a patchwork quilt posthaste. I also developed a rather nice line of stuffed elephants, but these were too large to be airmailed successfully.

Spurred on by Lois's success at Field 40, I suggested to Naomi that we might try the idea nearer to home and visit her family at Tavakubu village. A week later we set off, macrame string and embroidery threads to hand.

Despite the havoc wrought by modernisation and Western influences, most Fijian villages were still fairly traditional. A few decades previously, the traditional Fijian village had been a wonderful sight to behold. These days, in the name of progress, corrugated iron forms most roofs, replacing the thatch of old. As soon as the family can afford it, wood or concrete replaces what were once beautifully hand-woven walls. Now, it seems that the ultimate aim of everyone but the staunchest traditionalist is to own a concrete house. This was brought home to me when Naomi's uncle offered her a plot of land at Tavakubu and I expressed my delight at being able to visit her in her own bure (house). "Oh Marama," she cried, "I can't build a traditional house using just materials from the forest, or everyone will think I am poor."

Most Fijian villages have been built near water. For centuries, the lives of the villagers have been tied up with the sea, and although few are still self-sufficient, many dream of ending their days back home on one of the outer islands, spear fishing and growing dalo and bananas. Even back in 1976, some villagers still washed their clothes in the river, beating them with sticks and draping them over the bushes to dry in the hot sun. On many occasions, even my Naomi resorted to basics, ignoring the rotary washing line and drying her sulus over the shrubs in our garden.

But, back to our visit to the village for crafting.

I had met several of Naomi's extended family before, either when they visited her flat or at the market, so as I removed my shoes and entered her auntie's bure, I felt quite at home.

Nothing ever prepares you for the sheer warmth of a Fijian welcome. As soon as you enter a home, you are made to feel as though you are a special and very welcome guest. If you are lucky, a yaqona or kava ceremony is held in your honour. Throughout Fiji and most of Polynesia, the drinking of yaqona (kava or grog) is a common social custom. The ground powder is made from the root of the pepper plant, and I soon learnt the tradition of taking a gift of these plants whenever I visited a Fijian home. A lot of Fijian Indians have also adopted the habit.

The root is pounded in a type of mortar and pestle, and once the grit has been removed by straining through a muslin-type cloth, the liquid is ready to drink.

It is served from a tanoa, which is a large wooden bowl beautifully carved from hardwood. More often nowadays, it is made in just a large, thick, plastic bowl.

The guest of honour is then handed a bilo - a half coconut shell - with a great ceremony. Holding this before him in both hands, he drinks the murky grey liquid in a single draft, whereupon there is a cry of "Maca" pronounced "maatha," meaning "it is drained" accompanied by a clapping of hands. The rest of the assembled party then follows suit, drinking in order of rank. The first time I tried kava it came as a bit of a shock; the dirty-looking liquid appeared very unappealing and it left a slight tingling in my mouth. Now, however, I thoroughly enjoy the whole thing and can drink many bowls in one sitting with no ill effects!

How badly I digress. Close friends always say it takes me an hour to tell a five-minute story and I guess this book proves it.

To return to Naomi's auntie.

After being warmly welcomed into her home, I was given a gift of the most beautifully woven mat about four metres in length. Knowing just how long this would have taken her to make, and that prior to my visit it had probably been intended as a gift for a wedding or other celebration, I was embarrassed at first to be offered such a treasure. I was told that I must accept it, as I was the very first white lady to have entered her home and she was so delighted that she wanted to mark the occasion. I felt close to tears and very humbled, as I was on so many occasions during my time in Fiji. These warm and generous people, who had so little materially, always shared whatever they could. Over the years, I became the recipient of many beautiful handcrafted items; in fact, towards the end of my stay I learnt not to outwardly admire a Fijian's possessions, or they would probably make you a gift of them.

There is an old tradition in Fiji, known as *kerekere,* and I was to learn about this quite unexpectedly. One day, after Naomi had been with me for a couple of months, she arrived upstairs to begin work, wrapped in a blanket.

Assuming she was feeling cold, I passed no comment, but as the morning wore on I could resist no longer.

"Naomi, are you feeling cold?"

"No, Marama."

"Why are you wearing a blanket then?"

"Because I don't have any dresses left."

"Oh. But you had lots of dresses yesterday and you wore that lovely green one to church."

"Yes Marama, but then my sisters and cousins came to visit and they kerekere'd them."

Further investigation revealed the sad truth.

According to this ancient custom, if a friend or family member covets and admires any of your possessions, you are obliged to give them away. Naomi, being somewhat of a traditionalist as well as a caring and Christian woman, believed in this system wholeheartedly but rarely claimed anything herself. This time, she appeared to have been a little too generous!

Realising that the problem was likely to recur, we hit on a solution. We went to town and bought lots of material. Some of it we made up into everyday dresses and sulus, which would hang in Naomi's room and be available for kerekere. The nicer fabrics we made would stay upstairs in my wardrobe, out of the sight of acquisitive eyes. This system proved to be quite satisfactory, although I think at times, Naomi had to do some pretty smooth talking to explain the absence of certain desirable dresses they had seen her wearing at church!

Having dispensed with the social niceties, we settled down to work. Initially there were just four of us (myself, Naomi, and Naomi's auntie and cousin) crafting in the village, but as word got around, our numbers swelled to include various aunts, cousins, and friends. Sitting on the floor, we exchanged ideas. One lady had designed some super cushions, so we all decided to copy those and the bure was soon filled to the brim with triangles of red, white, and blue material. Despite their lack of English and my inability to understand much Fijian, we managed to communicate well. Naomi was an excellent translator. She had only had a few years of official schooling, but was remarkably intelligent and had an amazing grasp of English and Hindustani, in addition to understanding several dialects in her native Fijian language. The women were amazed to find that I too could weave mats, fans, and bags in the traditional manner, using leaves from the voi voi tree. Naomi had spent many hours teaching me this skill, and although my results were crude and rather tatty, we were both proud of my progress and delighted to show off my pièce de résistance - a misshapen but lovingly made woven shopping basket. Embroidery was a great favourite too, and whilst I worked on my boring old brown and gold bird pictures, the others were producing the most beautiful brightly-coloured pillow cases, emblazoned with the names of brides and grooms to be.

A Fijian wedding is the cause for great celebration, and I was delighted to be invited to Ratu Meli and Sarah's.

Ratu Meli was Naomi's nephew, a charming young man who had worked very hard at school and was by then a junior librarian at the Western Regional Library in Lautoka. I knew him quite well because he often came to visit at our house, and I was such an avid reader that I usually bumped into him at least twice a week when I went to change my library books.

He and Sarah were to make their home in the little flat adjoining the library, and it was decided that the wedding party would be held there as it was very conveniently placed near town, with the church just across the road.

Naomi and her family were Methodists and attended church every Sunday, the men and boys looking extremely smart in black or brown sulus with white shirts and dark ties, while the ladies wore bright and colourful dresses with underskirts of contrasting colours. On Sundays, the church would often be packed to overflowing, almost as if the entire Methodist population of Western Viti Levu had descended on the building. Loudspeakers had to be erected outside to reach those unable to squeeze inside, and until the arrival of the Hare Krishna movement (more on this soon), the church certainly seemed to be the most well-supported religious establishment in Lautoka.

There is a great diversity of religion in Fiji, not long established and dating back only to the middle of the 19th century when the missionaries first came to the islands. Consequently, whole villages were converted according to the various beliefs of those early missionaries, and so there became flourishing churches of Methodists, Roman Catholics, Baptists, Anglicans, and Seventh Day Adventists. Today, there are even more as is common with the rest of the world; religion is now big business and there are many new offshoots.

The arrival in Fiji of the Hare Krishna movement in the late 1970s caused quite a stir. Young, saffron-robed American men roamed the streets of Lautoka, chanting and enticing passers-by to join them. Obviously the large Hindu population welcomed their arrival, and in no time at all an enormous temple was erected on Tavewa Avenue, complete with a small school, restaurant, and gold-plated domes. It became so popular that special buses would bring worshippers from out of town. They had an open day and Naomi and I attended, but she was most distressed that, although they had gold-plated domes, there were not any chairs for the congregation to sit and worship. She decided that hers was a much more satisfactory religion!

But, back to the wedding.

It had been due to begin at 2 o'clock in the afternoon, so Naomi and I, Semesa, Jo, and Ma set off after lunch, laden down with wedding presents and food for the party. We arrived to find the library yard a hive of activity.

Assorted female relatives were busily preparing a feast. As each guest arrived, they would present their contribution... a chicken, pork, fish cooked in coconut milk, dalo, pineapples, or whatever else they brought to share. By the time the last guest appeared, the mountain of food was enormous and everyone was getting hungry just looking at it.

Ratu Meli and Sarah were busy helping too, and no one seemed concerned at all that the hours were ticking by. Naomi kept trying to reassure me that "in a minute we will start the wedding," but having lived among these lovely people for some time now, I realised that punctuality was not generally something they considered too important. Besides, I was having a wonderful time playing with all the children and just soaking up the atmosphere. Just before 5 o'clock, the minister from the church popped over to see how we were getting on. He was a charming Polynesian gentleman, much respected by his congregation, and when he gently reminded us that we were three hours overdue, everyone jumped up, dusted themselves down, took the last pan of dalo off the cooker, and followed him over the road to the church. In a simple but very moving ceremony, Ratu Meli and Sarah were finally married. She looked very beautiful in a simple dress enhanced with traditional tapa cloth (hand painted cloth, made from the bark of the mulberry or masi tree).

As soon as the ceremony was over, we all followed the minister back to the library yard to begin celebrating in earnest. I can honestly say that despite all the hanging around and the lateness of the hour - it gets dark very early in Fiji, so it always seems later than it is - that wedding was as enjoyable as any I have attended anywhere in the world, before or since.

Because of the diversity of its people, there was always some celebration or another taking place in Fiji. Mostly these were religious festivals, although we did have more than our fair share of public holidays. We even had a day off for both the Queen and Prince Charles's birthdays, which didn't even happen in England.

Christmas and Easter were important of course, although Christmas in the tropics was not quite the same as my Christmases of the past. When friends and family sent Christmas cards from England, Naomi would spend ages looking at them; one day, after studying a snow scene, she asked if the snow hurt when it fell on your head.

Although the climate was very temperate, we did suffer some extremes of weather on the islands.

The first time we had a "big rain," I could not believe my eyes.

Naomi and I were out on one of our regular jaunts. When we left home it was a typical day, hot and sunny, ideal for the skimpy little cotton dresses we were wearing. Within just a few minutes, the heavens opened and we were engulfed in the fiercest rainstorm I had ever seen. Drenched to the skin, we ran back to the car, where I collapsed in a soggy heap whilst Naomi merely shook her curly hair to get rid of the excess moisture and sank elegantly back into her seat. Within half an hour or so, the rain had stopped completely and the roads began to steam. This was my first introduction to this weather phenomenon, and once I was used to it, I longed to throw caution to the wind and join Jo and Ma when they sat in the gutter and let the rain pour over them. They felt it was a great improvement on the baths and showers their mother forced them to endure.

Over the years, Fiji has suffered very badly from the havoc wrought by hurricanes. Entire villages had been wiped out and many families have to rebuild their houses year after year. Nowadays, the hurricane warning systems are very efficient, and the local radio and television stations advise of forthcoming winds well in advance. It was not always this way.

I had been in Fiji for about six months when we had our first hurricane.

We were advised to stock up on tinned food and candles and then to stay at home. Businesses were closed and we had to remove all pictures and ornaments from the walls and stick tape across the windows. We selected the bathroom as the most suitable shelter as it had no big windows, and settled down for the duration of the storm. It was very frightening as we sat there all night, playing cards and drinking coffee from the flasks that Naomi and I had prepared. The wind whistled around the house and we could hear the windows rattling in their frames.

In the morning, the radio gave the all clear and we emerged to find such desolation. The street was littered with debris, some of it blown from the roofs of houses several blocks away, and our garden was devastated. The avocado tree was uprooted from the ground, all the coconut and banana trees were destroyed, and my beautiful frangipanis looked as though a giant fist had broken them systematically, branch by branch. I was heartbroken, but Naomi said, "Don't worry Marama, we'll just stick them back in the ground to grow again." Fancying myself as something of a gardener, I tried to explain that it wouldn't work as they had no roots left, but she persisted and I didn't have the heart to argue. Lo and behold, just a few short weeks later, there were frangipani shoots everywhere and our garden had begun to return to its former glory. The rest of the city suffered quite badly as well; lots of business premises were damaged, losing their roofs and windows. However, the mainland was lucky compared to some of the outer islands, which were completely devastated.

If I hadn't already known it, this experience would have taught me that the Fijian people are amazingly resilient. They suffer these disasters year after year, and although some still believe in the superstitions of their traditional culture, they also talk of acts of God and God's will. This faith has helped them to cope with the cultural and environmental changes in their society.

New Year was also celebrated in a big way, as everyone dressed in their best and some paraded the streets, draped in tinsel and long balloons. As midnight struck, drums were banged and water was thrown to wash away the old year; if you were wise, you avoided being anywhere near a swimming pool or water for a few days or you would get thoroughly soaked!

My two years in Fiji drifted along in a very pleasant way.

Richard was very busy with his job, and much of his spare time was filled with playing cricket, snooker, and Hash House Harriers. In theory this was a running club, but apparently one of their aims was to down as much Fiji Bitter as possible after each run.

I was thoroughly enjoying my first break from full-time employment, although I missed my monthly salary dreadfully.

In addition to my little outings and committee meetings, I learnt to play squash, tried desperately to improve my swimming (with no real success I am ashamed to report), and became a beachcomber.

Members of Naomi's family would often come to stay with her, and before they left to return to their home island they would always come upstairs to thank me for the water they had used for washing and showering. Piped water was not commonplace in many outlying villages, in those days and they seemed to really appreciate the comparative luxury of Naomi's flat. Often, they would leave me a small gift of a shell, and once it became known that I was starting a collection, they went out of their way to find me the biggest and best on the beach. In those far off days they even brought me some from the ocean, which is of course totally frowned upon now. To help identify the different varieties, I bought a little book entitled *Seashells of the World*, and from then on, Naomi would issue explicit instructions to her family as to which shell they should bring me next. Consequently, I ended up with the most wonderful collection... and a sore back, from walking along every beach with my head down looking for treasures.

Occasionally, we would take a trip to one of the outer islands.

These journeys took us past lots of tiny and uninhabited atolls; sitting on the boat, basking in the hot tropical sun, I dreamt of doing a Robinson Crusoe.

Arriving on Castaway or Mana, Beachcomber Island, or wherever, I could hardly wait to jump ashore and stroll along the white, sandy beach, dipping my toes in the crystal clear warm water - not forgetting to beware of sea snakes.

Coral viewing was the "thing to do" but having donned flippers, a snorkel, and a mask, I very quickly decided that with my limited swimming skills and fear of the water, it was not really for me. I retreated instead to the comfort of a glass-bottomed boat. The first time, in company with a nice American family, we whizzed out and quickly reached the reef. The engine was stilled and we settled down to watch. Apart from an occasional childish shriek of "Mom, is that a shark?" we were silent, watching the beautiful scene that unfolded before our eyes: shoals of vividly coloured fish in shades of mauve, yellow, blue, black, and white. The coral was a sight to behold as well, in delicate hues of white, beige, yellow, blue, mauve, pink, and red. It was utterly fascinating, and I realised that all the Jacques Cousteau documentaries I had seen were not exaggerated.

There are a lot of very beautiful beaches in Fiji, but my favourite on the mainland was Natadola. Situated on the Coral Coast between Nadi and Sigatoka and in those days only accessible by way of a dirt track, it was nearly always deserted. I felt so happy there and at that time, it was undoubtedly the nearest thing to heaven I had yet encountered. Shell hunting was quite successful here, and because it was quiet, I could march up and down the beach, singing hymns to my heart's content. These days it is quite different; while still a very beautiful beach, it now has several hotels and lots of tourists to spoil the calm.

Even though I was enjoying my time, I was still longing to have babies of my own. Despite suggestions from well-meaning friends that I should "just forget to take the pill and go ahead, because he'll love the baby once it arrives," I again agreed to a temporary postponement of our plans for parenthood. I was very lucky because there were always beautiful little Fijian babies around to cuddle, and Naomi's sisters and cousins often lent me their offspring for the afternoon. I loved to read or play games with them and hug their warm little coconut-scented bodies, and it made up a little for the lack of my own children. Sometimes, I would spend the hot sunny afternoons on the balcony, reading a book or working on my embroidery.

When school ended for the day, lots of kids trooped past our house on their way home. They were a splendid sight in their lilac and white uniforms; if they saw me they always stopped and waved.

They were much happier though if I was nowhere to be seen, for then they would rush up the drive and steal mangoes from our tree. I didn't mind this at all; I could remember scrumping apples in exactly the same way as a child, but if Naomi spotted them she would charge down the drive, yelling like a raging bull and sending them all scurrying away.

Naomi treated Jo and Ma, her very own sons, in exactly the same way if she found them eating a mango without permission. This was not because she was in the least bit mean, but because she had an ulterior motive. I had told her that any surplus fruit was hers to sell at the market or to give to her friends if she wished, and there was always a need for extra cash. The boys needed new books for school, or her parents were running short on kerosene for their lamp.

By now, our family was growing fast. Jo and Ma were doing well at school and Naomi's younger sister, Taina, was now living with us too, having passed her exams at school and secured a job at the local Northern Club. Salusalu, another of Naomi's sisters, came to stay from the island quite often, as did Naomi's lovely parents. A third sister, Nasau, who worked next door, had just given birth to another baby, so the house was almost always filled to overflowing and I never felt alone.

I had also made some friends amongst the expat community, mostly girls like myself whose husbands were on a two-year contract with different organisations. Among these were Leonie, Lindsay, and Christine from New Zealand, Adele and Barry from Australia, and Laurel from Rhodesia (now Zimbabwe). I had initially aimed for a much wider circle of acquaintances among the expat community, finding the social and cultural differences very interesting, but was very soon to realise that Richard had no real desire to mingle and certainly no intention of taking me to the club dances or social nights.

Of course I could have made a fuss, taken a stand and gone alone, but I did not want to cause a rift. Consequently, I spent many Friday and Saturday nights dancing at home, all by myself, whilst my new expat friends bopped the night away at the Northern Club and Richard perfected his snooker at the local men's-only sportsman's club.

As always, there were compensations to distract me.

Richard had many business functions to attend, and occasionally I would be invited to join him at a lunch or dinner. These were usually held in smart, expensive hotel restaurants, only fueling my desire to become more sociable. Sometimes he would have to go to Suva, the capital city, and once or twice I went along too.

Although Viti Levu is the largest island in the Fiji group, it is only about 170 miles from one side to the other along the Queens Road. It is easy to fly from Nadi to Suva, just a 30-minute trip, but I much preferred to drive when I got the chance, even though at that time, the sealed tarmac road ended just past the Coral Coast and the rest of the journey was on little more than a dirt track. There were such wonderful contrasts of scenery along this journey - miles of sugar cane fields and tiny Indian settlements with shiny white temples, then remote Fijian villages, where all the children rushed out of their houses to wave and stare at you as you passed. Women and children bathed in the rivers whilst white-haired matriarchs took care of their grandchildren. One minute you were passing beautiful deserted beaches scattered with chunks of coral and fallen coconuts, the next, you found yourself in what seemed like a lonely jungle forest with not a human soul in sight. Encompassed in that journey was everything that made Fiji enchanting to me.

Arriving in Suva was equally exciting, but for quite a different reason.

It was then home to some 60,000 people and the capital city of the Fiji archipelago. It was, by contrast to Lautoka, a cosmopolitan and bustling city. There were docks large enough to berth the QE2 and other large cruise ships when they arrived laden with tourists, and enough unloading areas for all the island produce of copra, banana, and yagona.

At Government House, the Changing of the Guard ceremony took place every four weeks and there were five cinemas if one fancied seeing a movie. There was no television at that time in Fiji, just the local radio station, with its Fijian, Hindi, and English programmes.

There were dozens of shops in Suva, mostly small and Indian-owned, and difficult to browse in without being pestered, but once it had been ascertained that I was indeed a local and not a rich tourist, I was generally allowed to wander freely. Fabrics were very cheap and mostly imported, and I bought lengths of silky material to make into sundresses. Having spent most of my money, I then wandered happily around the city, sometimes dropping into the market down by the wharf where Fijians, Indians, and Chinese jostled to sell their wares: fruit, vegetables, spices, fish, or local handicrafts and artifacts. Sometimes I would purchase a wooden carving here, a beautifully-woven bag there, and a big pile of pineapples or bananas. Then I would stagger back to the hotel, laden down with all my purchases. Richard would still be at work, so I would decide to retire somewhere interesting for a much-needed drink.

By now, I was confident enough to saunter into even the grandest hotel and order myself a drink. I never was and probably never will be a great drinker, but I do love the atmosphere of a smart establishment. The Grand Pacific Hotel in Suva became a favourite of mine, and after sipping my expensive little cocktail I would wander out onto the balcony, where the Queen of England had stood to wave to the crowds on her state visit just a few weeks previously.

Whilst in Suva, I also managed to fit in a visit to the Fiji Museum in Thurston Gardens. Erected in the early 1900s, it was like a little piece of England, with pretty gardens, summerhouses, and fountains with cherubs. The museum itself was fascinating - lots of very old, rather gruesome pictures of the local cannibals, along with forks used to eat the cooked, human flesh. There were old spears, masks, and even an old Bible that dated back to the 1860s, when King Cakobau decided to become a Christian and stop eating people.

All of a sudden, time started to run out.

Richard's work permit was expiring fast, and having achieved the work he had been sent out to do, his job was being localised. There was no possibility of an extension.

I was heartbroken, for I had really come to love this country and her people, and was certainly not looking forward to returning to cold old England, despite the fact that I would see my much loved family again. But, sentiments aside, plans had to be made.

Naomi had decided that she was to be a homeowner and she could think about retiring from house-girl duties, instead seeking a job as a ward maid at the hospital. It was a much sought after position, for although the hours were long and the work very hard, it was comparatively well paid. On that basis, we had to make sure that her new house at Tavakubu was completed and ready to move into before we left for England.

To raise some extra cash to buy the materials, Semesa did our gardening and repainted the outside of the house. I chose a bright pink paint which I thought rather fabulous, but some of my friends and neighbours didn't really approve of such frivolity and much preferred the original, a boring cream colour.

Gradually, the car port began to fill up with piles of timber and roofing tin.

Semesa sometimes worked as a docker, but as there was often no work available down at the wharf, he was able to devote a lot of time to the building of their house.

One afternoon, Naomi and I drove down to see how it was progressing. I was amazed to see several men from the village carrying enormous lengths of bamboo. Apparently, they had cut it down from the forest the previous day.

Semesa was wearing thick gloves and very skilfully weaving these lengths into walls for the house. I was fascinated, and, much to the amusement of the men to whom of course it was quite commonplace, I persuaded Naomi to stay for a while and watch.

We were due to leave Fiji at the end of July, and at the beginning of that month, Semesa invited me to Tavacubu to view the finished result.

I had to fight very hard to hold back tears that day. That little house had been so lovingly constructed. He had even made Naomi little bookshelves to house her Bible and my old earmarked copies of Time Life magazine. The brightly-coloured curtains that she had laboured over hung proudly at the windows, and there were new embroidered pillowcases and mats on the table. "One day," said Semesa, "I shall build on a kitchen." I just wished that I was rich enough to give them all the help they needed and so richly deserved. Sadly, having no job, I was totally reliant on Richard for any money, and he was not quite as generous towards others as I was.

My last two months in Fiji were quite hectic.

I had to arrange the packing and shipping of our possessions back to England and this proved to be quite a mammoth task, as by now I had acquired so many treasures. You may recall that we arrived with just four suitcases, and when I mention that the enormous crate finally shipped back took four strong men to lift it, you can perhaps appreciate the size of my collections.

There were several farewell parties and coffee mornings given on my behalf, and I was very sad to leave these friends. Mostly though, I dreaded leaving my own Fijian family, and Naomi and I had to stop discussing it for it always ended in tears.

Taina was going to be twenty-one just before we left Fiji, and when Naomi asked if they could hold the party in our garden I was delighted, even though I knew it meant digging up the garden to make a lovo (underground oven).

The day before the party, folk started to arrive. They came from far and wide, the whole extended family from Naviti Island in the Yasawas. In those days, it was a very uncomfortable and rather dangerous six- or seven-hour journey on a tiny boat, quite different from the short and easy trip on the Yasawa Flyer which today's locals and tourists undertake. Cousins, aunts, and uncles arrived from their homes in remote villages elsewhere, and they all settled down in the carport sitting cross-legged on woven mats, to drink kava and discuss all the family news.

They had also brought a pig from the island, quite the ugliest pig I had ever seen - more like a wild boar - greyish in colour with lots of coarse hair. He was securely tied to the mango tree, and both Dingo the dog and Marmalade the cat were terrified and avoided him like the plague.

In the morning he was gone, together with most of the overnight guests.

Later that afternoon I sat in the garden, watching Naomi and her mother weave banana leaf baskets. These were to hold the food during cooking in the lovo.

"What are we going to be eating later?" I asked Naomi.

"Oh, just dalo, fish, chicken, pork, and the usual things, Marama," she replied.

"Naomi, where is the pork coming from?" I had suddenly realised the truth.

"Oh, Semesa and my father have just cut its throat, so it will be ready for the lovo in a minute."

My heart sank. I would have given anything to have that poor, ugly old pig safely back under our mango tree, but I couldn't express such a soppy sentiment for I knew they had been saving him for such an occasion and I had no wish to spoil their pleasure.

I couldn't bear to watch as they dug an enormous hole in the ground and prepared the lovo. Into it they gently lowered the prepared pork, together with cassava, potatoes, and all the other party fare, and then left it to cook slowly while they organised the rest of the festivities.

Taina looked beautiful that evening. She was a pretty girl anyway, but dressed in traditional tapa cloth, her perfumed skin glistening with coconut oil, she could easily have passed as a princess from days long ago.

Suddenly it was here - the day I had rather hoped would never come.

Naomi and I were both quite hopeless. Every time we looked at each other, we burst into tears. In the end, Richard just packed us in the car together with Marmalade the cat, for the final journey to Tavacubu.

At the end we were all in tears: Naomi, Semesa, Jo, Ma, Taina, SaluSalu, Nasau, Naomi's mum, Naomi Junior, Maseke, and I. Only baby Moses remained dry-eyed.

I just could not bear to think that I would never see these dear people again and that the rest of my life would not include them.

It was with a very heavy heart that I boarded the plane bound for Los Angeles.

BACK TO MY OLD LIFE

I spent most of the long flight alternating between retaining a British stiff upper lip and giving in to my true feelings, degenerating into a red-eyed soggy mess. I missed my beloved Fijian family already.

As we began the downward descent into LA airport, my spirits rose a little and my natural excitement and joy in life overtook my sorrow. At last, I was going to meet Mickey Mouse! Since I was a tiny girl I had loved that cartoon character, despite my fear of the real version. Therefore, it had long been my ambition to go to Disneyland. We planned to spend three or four days in L.A. but had not taken the precaution of booking any accommodation in advance, and as it was late July and peak holiday season, this caused a little problem.

None of the hotels we rang on the airport courtesy phone had any rooms available (this was years before the internet and a click of a button to secure a room), so we hopped into the nearest cab and asked the driver to find us somewhere reasonably-priced to stay. 'Round and 'round downtown we drove, but there was no room for us anywhere. Night was closing in when we finally found sanctuary. It was definitely not in the best area and had certainly seen better days, but at that time of night, even a seedy oasis was better than nothing.

The Mexican night porter paused just long enough to take his eyes from his chilli hot dog to point a grubby, ketchup-stained finger at the lift, directing us to the 13th floor. The lift and all the corridors were emblazoned with framed photographs of movie stars, all signed and supposedly in recognition of wonderful times spent in that illustrious establishment. One could only assume that the place had been a little more splendid in the days when Buster Keaton, Marilyn Monroe, and Clark Gable had visited. Our room matched the rest of the hotel - peeling gold-flocked wallpaper, cracked hand basin, smoke-stained ceilings, and very noisy neighbours. But at least the sheets were reasonably clean, and while Richard spent the remainder of the night fiddling with the three hundred odd channels on the flickering television, I dozed fitfully, crying every time I thought about all my loved ones in Fiji and trying not to think about bed bugs.

The next morning, it was all different.

I just loved Los Angeles. This was my first trip to the States, and I was determined to experience *everything*. After the relative confines of my beloved Fiji, I couldn't wait to roam the wide, noisy streets, although my enthusiasm almost got me arrested for jaywalking as I unintentionally ignored the "Walk" and "Don't Walk" signs. I spent hours in the huge department stores, not spending any money but simply feasting my eyes on all the Western decadence I had missed for the last two years. I had to tear myself away to meet Richard back at the bar adjoining the hotel, where he had spent a happy hour or two watching American football on the outsized TV screen while developing a taste for Budweiser beer. This was the 1970s, and such exotic things were not readily available in England then. And of course, there had been no television at all in Fiji. Then it was over the road to Joey's Deli for a custom-made sandwich: rye bread stuffed with thick slices of beef, salads of twenty-seven varieties, and lashings of mayonnaise, all carefully secured with a pink cocktail stick! During the hot, steamy afternoons, we ventured into slightly seedier areas downtown; although you could sense some tension and would not necessarily want to visit there once night had fallen, it was fascinating to find such a melting pot. Mexicans rubbed shoulders with Blacks, whilst sad-looking Eastern European immigrants laden with brown paper sacks full of grocery shopping struggled home to dingy apartment blocks.

There were makeshift shoeshine stalls set up beside the road, and one, run by a very handsome young Black boy, seemed to be doing much better business than the rest. Always interested in success stories, I wandered over and was amazed to find all his customers reading pornographic magazines. Obviously, he believed in offering his clientele something a little more interesting than old copies of Time Out.

A whole day was put aside for my trip to Disneyland.

We took a bus from downtown and as we drove into the Magic Kingdom parking lot, my excitement almost unbearable.

After paying the required amount to give you a carte blanche ticket to pleasure, we entered the gates and I, together with 90% of the other visitors, became a child again. I firmly believe that everyone, if they so desire, should have the chance to visit Disneyland at least once in their lives. It is such a magical experience and unless you are a total cynic, you cannot fail to be just a little enchanted.

At the end of a very exciting day, during the Grand Parade down Main Street, I sat on the edge of the pavement with all the other kids and wept unashamedly when Mickey Mouse appeared, dancing and waving before my very eyes.

I so enjoyed our brief stay in L.A., but all too soon it was over. This time though, there were no tears, for I was determined that one day I would return to explore more of this fascinating country.

Boarding yet another plane, my thoughts turned to England and a reunion with my family. We had corresponded of course during my two year absence, but apart from a visit from my little sister Carol, I had not seen or spoken to them at all, as Mum and Dad did not have a phone at home. Would they have changed much? Could I just slot back into their lives as if I had never been away?

These and many more questions were buzzing around inside my head as we waited for our luggage to appear on the carousel at Heathrow. Our cases arrived safely this time and after whizzing through customs, I headed for the exit, pausing just briefly en route to buy an essential item.

You may recall that chocolate has always been something of a passion of mine, but during my two-year stay in Fiji, for reasons of availability rather than choice, I had barely indulged and thought myself quite cured of this disgusting habit. It says much for my self-discipline and self-control when I confess that within ten minutes of landing back in England, I was happily indulging in a Mars Bar.

After spending a few happy days renewing ties with my lovely family, who, of course, had not changed at all - although Mum and Dad did seem to have gotten smaller - it was time to return home to Aldershot.

Our house had been rented to Richard's company during our absence, and apart from my pretty little garden being rather overgrown and a few cobwebs, nothing had really changed. Within a week or two, it was hard to imagine I had ever been away. To calm my homesickness, for home was certainly how I now thought of Fiji, I donned overalls and prepared to decorate the house from top to bottom, hoping this would make me feel more settled. When our crate finally arrived from Fiji, I unpacked it in floods of tears. Even the old copies of the Fiji Times, which were wrapped around my shell collection, seemed infinitely more interesting to me than the Daily Telegraph, Times, or Daily Mail.

Once that was all dealt with, I sadly accepted that that part of my life was gone forever and I forced myself to concentrate on the future. The only time I really digressed was when I undressed at night. I would throw my clothes in a heap on the floor, only to realise a few days later that if I didn't pick them up, they would stay there forever. No Naomi to clean up after me now.

Richard returned to his old job, but very soon it became apparent that he too was unsettled and yearned to try something different.

By now, my desire to have a baby was becoming desperate, but I realised that until he had found his niche, it would be silly to persuade Richard into fatherhood. Once again, I smothered my maternal instincts and returned to be a servant of Barclays Bank.

This time I worked at the Yorktown branch - near the Royal Academy in Sandhurst - and it was not long before I became very settled and happy there. I made several good friends amongst my new colleagues: Helen, Elaine, Linda, and Theresa, and together we enjoyed a good social life, both inside and outside of normal banking hours. Our manager, Dick Killick, was very involved with the local Lions Club and in the name of charity, we indulged in sponsored Pub Crawls, Race Nights, and Riverboat Shuffles.

Life ticked on; we became more affluent and installed patio doors, dishwashers, and automatic washing machines, but still no babies.

Finally, Richard admitted that he didn't really like babies much, and certainly had no real desire to father any of his own.

I was heartbroken. All my dreams turned to dust and I had to face a harsh reality. Either I continued to live with this man (whom I still loved) but without my longed-for children, or I left and started afresh.

After all, I was still only young at 29, and certainly not afraid to seek a new life alone. But I was very bound by love and loyalty, and when he suggested that we might consider adopting an older child, my fate was sealed. Instantly, I pictured myself as a mother of a five-, six-, or seven-year-old black, white, or green child. It mattered not, for I knew I was capable of loving almost anyone.

But first, the little matter of Richard's career.

By now we had come to realise that he found working for someone else rather disagreeable, so the only solution seemed to be a business of his own. Fortunately, we had managed to accumulate a little money during our time in Fiji, so this, together with a small early inheritance from my grandmother, provided enough capital to encourage the bank to loan us the remainder necessary to open our furniture shop.

Richard was very well qualified and determined, and our business proved reasonably successful. Within six months, we felt confident enough for me to resign from the bank. Not to be a mother sadly, but to become a full-time director, company secretary, and salesperson. I proved to be good, cheap labour, so parenthood plans were postponed yet again, although this time I did elicit a promise that we would apply to the adoption agencies before the year was out.

Apply we did, and after several months of in-depth interviews and visits from social workers, we were accepted as adoptive parents and put onto the waiting list.

Acting on their advice, I prepared a bedroom for this new addition to our family and filled it with books and toys suitable for a child of almost any age or background. I loved to wander into that little room, sit on the bed, and just anticipate the tinkling of childish laughter.

Again, at the suggestion of the social workers, I spent hours making up an album called a Life Book, chronicling a little of our family history with photos of all our immediate family and friends so that when our child finally appeared, they could get to know us a little before they came into our home. It all seemed so simple, and I knew that now the decision was made, I could wait patiently for my child to arrive.

Very unwilling to share the secret with all, we had just told our closest friends and of course my family. They were all very excited and I knew that Mum longed to be a grandmother to my children, whatever age or colour they might turn out to be. I realised that it could be a long wait, although hopefully not as long as for those couples who desperately wanted a healthy, white, newborn baby. In the meantime, I settled down to business and thoroughly enjoyed my new career.

The next two years passed quickly, and although I was anxious every day for news of my child, I learnt to be patient and was compensated by a busy, hectic business life. I visited factories and exhibitions and learnt all about making and selling furniture, beds, and carpets. I rediscovered my passion for interior design and was able to use it to great advantage in our one, and later two, modern furniture shops. We travelled too, to the Greek islands, France, Italy, and back to the States, this time to sunny Florida, where I fell in love all over again with Mickey Mouse.

As time ticked by, I was glad that so few people knew about the adoption plans, for I could not have borne to be constantly questioned. I was very grateful that my family and friends rarely mentioned it, because inside I was raw with emotion. I could barely pass a happy family group without tears welling, and spending time with my friends and their children became a kind of torture.

Still, I managed to remain optimistic, and nothing prepared me for the bombshell to come.

On a sunny October morning, I received a letter from the adoption agency saying that "they did not, after all, feel that they would be able to find a child for us."

In hindsight, I can see that it was probably a wise decision on their part. Richard was not really excited by the prospect of fatherhood and I was probably far too idealistic. But at the time, such wisdom was not forefront in my mind, and for many months I was heartbroken.

Gradually, I began to realise that the gaps in my life had become too large to ignore. I had a beautiful home and an enviable lifestyle, but all the soft Italian leather sofas, revamped kitchens, and Mayfair hotel lunches in the world could not compensate for the loneliness I felt.

I still loved Richard, but that love had been eroded over the years by his infidelities; he was so busy building his social life of snooker and football that I often felt there was not enough room for me. A classic case of too much love and affection to give and no one around with the time or enthusiasm to accept it.

With a very heavy heart, I realised that I had to leave this marriage before I became a complete door mat.

I knew that I would be very unlikely to claim anything by way of a divorce settlement, as I had no wish to destroy the business we had worked so hard to build. Additionally, I had certainly no desire to provoke his temper with a long and drawn-out court battle, so plans had to be made.

Firstly, I needed to find a job to support myself. I was only 32 and had spent ten years in banking, so surely it wouldn't be too difficult to find something?

Luckily, it proved to be much easier than I expected, and in no time at all I had secured a position with one of the leading charities, Dr. Barnardo's.

The salary from this would give me just about enough to rent a small flat, so for the next four weeks I scoured the papers and visited all the local estate and letting agents, slowly becoming utterly despondent.

Cushioned by owning my own home for so long, I had not realised what miseries lie in store for those less fortunate. Immediately, it seems you are labelled as a second-class citizen and I was horrified to be shown around dingy attics and tiny musty rooms by greedy landlords.

Despairing at ever being able to find somewhere suitable and becoming more anxious to leave my marital home, I visited the agents for a third time and noticed details of a large flat available in Alton Town Centre. This was far enough away from Aldershot for me to make a clean break, but apparently it was only suitable for a family, as the landlords had no desire to rent it to a single person like myself in case of reckless behaviour and wild parties. When I eventually talked my way into an interview, I was amazed to find the landlord to be an acquaintance from business days. Fairly confident that I was not a hooligan and therefore unlikely to wreck the place, he allowed me to sign the contract then and there. I was absolutely delighted. It was a huge flat, and although the decoration was a bit tatty, I knew that I could knock it into shape in no time at all.

I do not propose to go into any detail about the final days of my marriage.

Although it was my decision to leave, I still felt totally devastated.

It is not easy to walk away from 14 years of marriage, whatever your reasons, and you certainly do not stop caring about someone just because you can't live with them anymore. I can now talk, and even joke about some of the bad bits, like the time he insisted we took a canoe out to sea in Fiji and I nearly drowned whilst he casually paddled back to shore on the upturned boat! When recounting this tale later to a friend, I jokingly mentioned that he had recently insured my life for one hundred thousand pounds - a small fortune all those years ago. Afterward, I found myself wondering if perhaps the fact that I had discovered just before leaving England that he had been having an affair with his secretary was linked in some way!

In hindsight, Richard and I were too young to get married when we did. We were both strong and ambitious, but in different ways.

I will always be incredibly sad that it didn't work forever. Marriage is a wonderful institution if you are with the right person.

STARTING AGAIN

As usual, I had wonderful plans for the redecoration of my new home.

The flat had originally been built for a caretaker and his family, and was really quite large with three bedrooms, an enormous kitchen/dining room, a lounge, and a cavernous room in the basement. It adjoined the assembly rooms in the little market town of Alton in Hampshire. Most weekends, I would be an uninvited guest at dances, wedding receptions, and concerts, as the sounds found their way through the walls into my home. I even knew when number 435 on the pink ticket had won the raffle prize!

Actually, I didn't mind these noisy intrusions at all. It was the first time in my life that I had ever lived alone, and it was good to know that there really was a world outside my four walls.

Having made the momentous decision to leave my husband, home, business, and many of my much-loved possessions, the rest was comparatively easy.

There were quite a few times when I felt really lonely and miserable and indulged in long weeping sessions, and I often cried myself to sleep at night thinking of what might have been. But I was determined not to get bitter, and tried terribly hard to just take each day as it came and not dwell too much on the past.

It was a bit of a struggle financially, however. My new salary with Barnardo's just about paid my rent, gas, and electricity bills, but there was not much left to live on. For the first six months, I seemed to exist almost entirely on baked beans on toast and tins of Ambrosia creamed rice, supplemented by the occasional food parcel from Mum.

I was determined that, impecunious or not, my flat would be somewhere I could be really proud of, and to that end I began to study paint charts and fabric samples. Having made my choices, I set off on a spending spree, using my credit card and the paltry amount of cash I had gotten from a local jeweller in exchange for my wedding and engagement rings. I returned home with paint, sweet pea duvet covers, and bright red bathroom accessories.

I bought an electric drill and taught myself to put up shelves and glass cabinets; I was a little wary when using this tool, and always made sure to wear my Wellington boots when drilling in case of electric shocks! I was so proud when my handiwork was finished.

Each room reflected my personality, but my absolute favourite was the bathroom.

When I moved in, it had been decked out with wallpaper of rather hideous, large brown flowers, with yards of black tiles surrounding the bath and basin. It was a gloomy and depressing room, and instantly I spotted the chance to fulfil yet another life-long ambition: possess a completely red room.

The finished effect, which if I am truly honest was not a prime piece of workmanship as I was in such a hurry to complete it, was warm and inviting. Red painted walls, red pictures, red towels, red and black carpet to match the black wall tiles, and even a red toothbrush and red lightbulb. I loved to spend hours in that room, and since I was too poor to have much of a social life, I indulged in at least three baths a day.

My new job with Barnardo's, which had been taken out of necessity, quickly became the main focal point of my life.

Employed by such a worthwhile charity, I, together with my new colleagues, had few objections to working the long hours that were required. In fact, for many months it was undoubtedly a saving grace. It gave me stability and precious little time to feel sorry for myself, and it also gave me a kind of social life just when I needed it most.

During the course of my work as a general fundraising organiser, I met some delightful people - most of whom had worked extremely hard in a voluntary capacity for the charity for many years. There was little Betty Hooker, Vicky Townsend, Kay King, and Mary and Bob Clark, as well as many others, too numerous to name. They were all very kind to me and I would often be invited into their homes as a welcome guest. Sometimes they would decide I was looking too thin, and invite me to stay for a meal. I am sure they never realised quite how grateful I was for the sustenance of their cottage pie, or that extra slice of their delicious sponge cake. Thank you, my friends.

These people, together with my new colleagues Margaret and Jacquie, helped me through a very difficult patch in my life.

The job gave quite a lot of room for personal initiative.

Provided you managed to raise a lot of money, nobody minded too much how you did it - just as long as it was ethical and legal. Consequently, in addition to the normal flag days and street collections, jumble sales and raffles, we all racked our brains for something a little different.

Jacquie ended up with a mounted police pantomime. Margaret arranged several Queen's Life Guard concerts, and I became a Red Devil for a day. Actually, that's not strictly true. I organised twenty other brave souls to spend a weekend at the Red Devils army barracks in Aldershot, and then they risked life and limb by parachuting from 2,000 feet to raise money while I stood safely on the ground and cheered them on.

Apart from my job, I was slowly rebuilding my life.

Just occasionally, whilst wandering 'round the supermarket trying to decide whether I could afford Heinz beans this week, or had to stick with the store's own brand for economies sake, I would laugh aloud at the bitter irony. Who would imagine that just a year ago, I had been wandering around Harrods waving my American Express card, without a real financial care in the world.

Richard and I were now officially divorced; he was happy again with a new lady, the business was still thriving despite my absence, and I could stop feeling quite so guilty about leaving him. I was very lucky to be blessed with several really good friends and a caring family, although I had now lost all my grandparents, so was very aware that nothing lasts forever. My family would often phone to see how I was coping with my new single state; my divorce had come as a shock to them all, as I had never told anyone that my marriage was anything less than perfect. Although they lived some distance away, it was good to think that they would hasten to my side if a crisis arose.

The years following my divorce passed quite pleasantly. I enjoyed entertaining my friends and often spent weekends at their homes. I had learnt by now to cope with my unfilled maternal instincts, and could happily spend hours playing with the offspring of others without too much envy. In fact, with numerous nieces, nephews, and godchildren at my disposal, I became a very indulgent auntie.

Having no children of my own to keep me occupied, I looked around for distractions.

Encouraged by my friend Margaret, I began to attend antique auctions; my elderly neighbours would chuckle as I struggled home, week after week, with tatty chests of drawers, tables, and chairs - relics of the past that had been eagerly exchanged for modern, fitted furniture. I developed a passion for old oak chairs, and having little or no restraint, I ended up with at least half a dozen, all needing refurbishment.

Alton had an auction house in its marketplace. The auctioneer and his assistants were so friendly and charming that there was a real family atmosphere to the place, and in no time at all I was completely hooked. They also ran a weekly produce auction, and sometimes I would go along to bid for eggs, chickens, vegetables, or fresh-cut flowers. Once, I bought an enormous fuschia plant for just one pound, but really struggled walking up the High Street back to my flat, as it was so big that the beautiful flowers completely obliterated my view!

Sadly, such bargains are no longer available. After trading for many years, the auction house finally closed down - just another victim of the times - and the valuable site was redeveloped.

Alton was such a lovely little English country market town when I first knew it back in the late 1960s, but there have been many changes over the years since. Jane Austen, the famous writer, lived for a time in the nearby village of Chawton, and she too would be very sad to see the rather faceless suburb it seems to have become, now with its regulation quota of banks, building societies, estate agents, and multiple retail stores.

After a few years, it was time to move on from Alton. I found myself in Hastings in East Sussex, a historic seaside town that I had last visited with Jen nearly twenty years earlier on our first youth hostelling holiday. This time, however, I had precious little time to sunbathe on the pebbly beach.

I was now employed by the Imperial Cancer Research Fund as a regional shops organiser. Initially, my patch was the whole of Kent and East Sussex, and I thoroughly enjoyed the challenge of seeking out empty properties and arranging for them to be revamped as high-class charity shops. I made some wonderful friends, particularly Valerie, the lovely lady who ran our regional office; she became my best friend/confidante/extra Mum. Then there were my colleagues Sue and Tricia; we had so much fun, often during pretty stressful working conditions, and I am delighted to say that all three of them are still my great friends now, more than 30 years later.

Each shop was set up to eventually be run by 30 or 40 volunteers, and I was responsible for training them to operate the electronic till, sort and price the donated goods, and do the window displays.

Although it was very hard work actually preparing a shop for opening, the compensations were tremendous and I loved getting to know the people with whom I worked. A lot of them had led such interesting lives and had wonderful stories to tell. Again, I felt as though I had made many new friends.

After all our hard work, we would have a grand opening with the mayor, a local celebrity, and the town crier in attendance. It was at this time that I had to relinquish responsibility for my "baby," and hand over the running of the shop to my very capable helpers whilst I moved on to organising the next one.

From this moment on, it was no longer really "my shop"; I was relegated to being simply a weekly visitor who was otherwise generally only called in for tea parties and the odd crisis.

My broken marriage had taken its toll, but I was determined not to become reliant on one man ever again for my emotional happiness. However, the idea of living as a happy divorcee and having at least six boyfriends who all spoilt me outrageously sounded rather appealing.

While it sounds marvelous, this little project never really got off the ground. I soon realised that I was neither devious nor resolute enough to keep one man, let alone six, dangling on a string.

My friends introduced me to prospective partners over time, and I became very seriously involved with one of them for a couple of years. He was a nice man, but it was too soon after my divorce and eventually, it became apparent to me that our relationship was not destined to last forever.

We'd had a lot of fun together, bought a house and travelled around the world with one another, even went back to my beloved Fiji for a brief visit after my absence of eight long years.

Once again, I had a choice. I could swallow my doubts and desires and remain in this comfortable and safe relationship where I knew exactly what the future would hold, or I could follow my instincts and end it quickly and kindly, while we were both still young enough to pick up the pieces.

Knowing me as well as you do by now, you will probably have guessed that I chose the latter course of action.

This time, I left behind a beautifully-decorated modern town-house. We had a joint mortgage on it but he had paid the lion's share of the deposit, so it seemed fair to let him stay. He was an honourable man, so I knew I would get a little money from it eventually.

Perhaps I was "seeking a romantic illusion," as my rejected suitor had bitterly said, but deep in my heart I was sure that somewhere in this world existed my Mr. Right. It was just a case of finding him.

It's funny how, just when you think you have your life sorted out, everything changes. So it was in my 41st year.

Since leaving Hastings, I had spent the past four and a half years living happily in Eastbourne with another lovely man, Andrew. I met Andrew at a service station, where he chatted me up after filling his car with petrol. In my usual optimistic fashion I was convinced it would be forever this time, but of course, after the first few years of everything being rosy - or at least pink-tinged - reality seeped in. I became aware of big differences between myself and this new partner.

Unfortunately, the biggest difference between Andrew and me was that he was a confirmed bachelor and I wanted commitment and children.

This is not an easy issue to resolve, particularly if you are having fun and the relationship works in so many other ways. He had been very honest with me right from the beginning about not wanting marriage or babies, but of course, I thought and hoped I could change his mind!

Andrew and I did loads of travelling together. America, the Bahamas, we went skiing several times in both France and Italy, skiing being a sport at which I was spectacularly bad, a real wimp, while he whizzed down the mountains with great speed. We went boating in Devon and Cornwall, again a great passion of his which I valiantly tried to enjoy despite my fear of boats and water. We played tennis, rode bikes, and at last, I achieved a life-long ambition and bought my own bike - a lovely old-fashioned red one with a wicker basket on the front.

A few months into our relationship, I became sick. No one was quite sure what was wrong; despite many tests and two hospital stays there was no conclusion, so I discharged myself. I had a dreadful pain in my rib area, which was really debilitating. Although I had suggested to every medical person who dealt with my case that perhaps I had just broken a rib, none of them took my views seriously and they continued to look for other causes. I was tested for cancers, kidney disease, and various viruses. It seemed to me that whatever a doctor's speciality was, that was what I was tested for.

There seemed to be no reprieve in sight, so I decided in my usual high-handed fashion that whilst loving my job, it was quite wrong for such an admirable charity to have to pay me long-term sickness benefit. I resigned.

I then spent the next year searching for a cure, trying everything from acupuncture to yoga, a highly expensive consultation with an orthopaedic surgeon thrown in for good measure. I pointed out to him exactly where my rib hurt and the fact that it was such a strange shape, but he announced that I "must have been born with it looking like that, or had it injured in a car crash." Needless to say, having advised him that I was actually quite vain and would certainly have noticed such a blight on my body, I duly paid his exorbitant fee and left him to his stuffy consulting room and polished walnut table!

Several weeks after this, a friend suggested that I visit her osteopath to try and obtain some relief from my constant pain. Unconvinced but willing to try anything, I went along - what a joy. He took one look at my body and, quite unprompted, announced that I had obviously broken a rib! A few visits and some manipulation later, I began to feel a bit better. Of course by then, I had already done the resignation thing, so earning some sort of living became an issue. I was living in Andrew's house and paying just a little rent, so luckily, my overheads were not too high.

For some time I had enjoyed visiting auctions, so this became my new plan. I would establish myself as a general wheeler dealer! To this end, I bought an old yellow ex-GPO van and set off on my new adventures.

For the remainder of that year I pottered happily, visiting various auction sales and buying assorted items. My plan was to resell them at great profit, but of course I came unstuck several times by buying things I loved and could not bring myself to pass onto another. I also made many bad purchases in my enthusiasm, on which I lost money. On the whole, however, I made a profit, had an enormous amount of fun, and just about managed to support myself. I also ended up with an even bigger teapot collection and a vast array of old oak chairs.

Andrew and I started up a property development company and we worked tirelessly renovating three old Victorian houses. I became quite an expert at taking enormous piles of builder's rubble to the council tip in my little yellow van. That van saw a lot of action, and even was driven on a skiing trip to France one year loaded down with a small Christmas tree and piles of presents.

But of course, all good things must come to an end. When Tony, my old boss at Cancer Research, contacted me to say my old job was re-available, I had to make a sensible decision and return to the world of proper, paid work.

In 1991, I was again working happily for Imperial Cancer Research and thoroughly enjoying my job. My title was now area retail manager and I had so many lovely volunteers that it was usually a joy to go to work. We had such fun running the shops and organising fashion shows and general fundraising, that the years passed quickly. But my personal life was not quite as successful.

Andrew realised that I needed more than he was prepared to commit to, so we sadly parted. I moved into one of the houses we had renovated, took on a huge mortgage, and turned it into a beautiful nest for a forty-something-year-old single woman.

He began a relationship with a neighbour, a Japanese girl who was nowhere near as complicated or demanding as me. She had no desire for marriage or children, and had plenty of money.

My little Victorian terraced house in Eastbourne was perfect. Just right for a single childless woman of a certain age.

Immaculate. Cream walls, cream furniture, cream carpets. Plenty of wardrobe space, even a separate wardrobe for shoes. *And* one for handbags.

Certainly no room nor desire for another permanent man.

Instead, I had a fabulous holiday in Egypt, which was somewhere I had dreamt of going since I was a little girl.

When I was young, I had found the idea of such an ancient civilisation utterly fascinating and stuck a poster of the pharaohs on my bedroom wall. When, a few months after parting from Andrew, I spotted cheap flights to Egypt, I didn't hesitate. Much to the horror of my family and friends, I set off all alone, for Luxor and the Valley of the Kings.

The whole two-week trip was wonderful, one of the best holidays of my life.

Walking one afternoon on my way back to the hotel from Luxor town, I met a 14-year-old Egyptian boy called Mohammed who invited me to his village to meet his family. The village, a mile or so from my hotel, was full of old mud-built houses and upon entering, I was greeted by dozens of excited smiling children. I sat on a bed with his four sisters - none of whom spoke a word of English - and watched a flickering black and white television whilst eating the pigeon that his mother had cooked for us.

The next day, Mohammed and his father, who was extremely charming, took me to a camel market. I went on the local ferry to the Valley of the Kings, avoiding other tourists as much as I could. I so wanted to experience the *real* Egypt.

I chatted with the locals, learning about Coptic Christians and how the Egyptians despised the Romans for desecrating their temples and relics. I sat and drank sweet tea with the local taxi drivers and flirted with many attractive men. I sailed with one of these men on his traditional boat, a felucca, on the Nile River, and was quite enjoying the trip until he mentioned the crocodiles.

In Luxor, I also had a brief but very romantic encounter with a handsome young Frenchman called Olivier. He was only twenty five years old and exceedingly charming, his attention did great wonders for my forty-year-old, rather broken heart.

My trip ended with a whistle stop trip to Cairo, where I visited the overcrowded and muddled but extremely fabulous Cairo Museum and saw all the treasures from Tutankhamun's tomb. I climbed inside the pyramids, posed with camels, and paid a late-night visit - all alone, much to my taxi driver's distress - to the Khan el-Khalili bazaar, where I sampled exotic perfumes and heady spices, and bought tiny glass bottles and beautiful mirrors.

I was very sad when the time came to board the plane and return to boring old Sussex.

However, life never stays dull for long, and within a few weeks my life was to change again forever.

I had lots of plans. More exotic travel, working hard, designing my new garden, and certainly no dating for the foreseeable future.

Olivier was planning to come over from Paris to visit me in just a few months, so I could easily wait for some affection 'til then.

Interestingly though, my friends had other plans for me.

Just a few weeks after my return from Egypt, a dinner party was arranged. On a wet and windy night when anyone with half a brain would have stayed at home with a glass of wine and a good movie, it happened.

The end of my single life.

His name was Graham, he was eight years my junior and another frustrated teacher, the same as my last two boyfriends. Another frustrated teacher with big dreams - not the dream of a wife, though.

It was only when he had driven me home and the two of us were running to my house, using his Barbour jacket as a shield from the rain, that we realised it had been a set up.

We saw each other a few times, both desperate not to get too involved, not to run the risk of getting hurt again. But, as they say in the movies, "this thing was bigger than both of us."

We were married just four months later, on a sunny August day at Eastbourne Town Hall.

I was very happy with my new young husband, despite my initial misgivings about marrying again. I was absolutely thrilled when I discovered I was pregnant.

This joy turned to such sadness though, when I miscarried our baby and felt as though my chance of having a child at last was just a distant dream.

Imagine my delight when, just a few months later, I found myself pregnant again. It seemed that even at my great age I was still quite fertile.

Everything was going well. I was flourishing, the doctor was pleased with our progress, and my baby's heart was beating strongly. I was so happy, loving the way my body was changing and getting fat.

After the risky first twelve weeks of gestation had passed, I was so proud, sharing the news with friends and family and looking forward to my future as a mum at last.

Going up to London to the Harris BirthRight Trust for an amniocentesis scan just seemed like the next step in my new adventure. Even if the test showed an abnormality, nothing was going to stop me from loving my baby. My doctor had detected a strong heartbeat just two days before, so all was well.

But when they began the scan, they realised that my baby had died inside me and I felt as though my world was falling apart for a second time. To lose two much-wanted babies in such quick succession was absolutely heart-breaking. I was 41 years old, and obviously, never destined to be a mother.

Of course, despite my utter desolation, life has to go on.

I went back to work and tried to concentrate on building a childless future with my lovely new husband.

Mostly I coped, although many, many tears were shed, especially when friends or family gave birth to beautiful babies and I had to smile and cuddle them while my heart was silently breaking.

They could find no medical reason for my losses, except perhaps for my advanced years, so I had to accept that my chances of motherhood were probably gone. This was in the days before IVF, donor eggs, and surrogacy were readily available, so I truly felt I had no more options to make this dream of mine come true.

In July 1993, we went to a friend's wedding. It was a very hot day and there was nowhere to sit, just a small, crowded marquee with no chairs. I felt pretty sick and couldn't wait for the speeches to be over so we could leave.

When we got home my instincts kicked in, and I found a pregnancy testing kit in the bathroom - my optimistic nature had not allowed me to throw them all away. Much to my joy and surprise, it was POSITIVE.

The next eight months passed in a flash, although I never really relaxed.

Every day, I expected to lose my much-wanted baby.

I would stroke my expanding tummy and tell Baby to stay safely curled up in there until it was time to be born. I sang, played soothing music, and talked constantly to my unborn child, just willing it to stay alive.

When I was six months pregnant, disaster struck.

Not in the form of a miscarriage this time, but a flood instead.

It was a wild and wet New Year's Eve, and certainly not a night when any sane pregnant person should be out driving. But my mother-in-law wanted a lift to the station.

Unfortunately, several roads were flooded, and I had to take a diversion through the Industrial Estate. It was dark, too dark to see the puddle, and by the time I realised anything was amiss, we were stuck.

Just like in the movies, the water came into the car so quickly that within minutes, the dirty cold water was up to our waists. The electrics in the car failed, and we were suddenly sitting there in complete darkness with no way of getting out. The doors would not open because of the pressure of water outside. By now, the water was more than five feet high; had it not been for the brave actions of a couple of passing men and a local policeman who managed to push the car back out of the deep water, the consequences would have been tragic. On being rushed to the local hospital to check out my baby, I was told that, had we been in the water for another ten minutes, my precious baby would have died.

Despite being caught in the flood and featured on the front page of the local newspaper, and thereafter being known as the woman carrying the Balcombe Flood Baby, all was well.

After being overdue for 10 days, then experiencing a long labour and emergency cesarean operation, my precious daughter, Lucy, was born on the 6th April 1994, weighing nine pounds, six ounces.

The best and most fulfilling part of my life had begun.

At the age of 43, I was a mother at last.

NEW BEGINNINGS

Apparently, I didn't stop smiling for months after Lucy's birth. It had been a bit traumatic initially; after she was safely born, I suffered a major hemorrhage and almost died, so we had to stay in the hospital for almost a week. I was terrified that someone would steal her, so I surrounded her cot with trolleys and flowers. On our final day there I had obviously relaxed, as I forgot about her and left her in her cot by the hot chocolate machine, only realising once I got back to the comfort of my bed.

Once at home, I couldn't do as much as I wanted, as I was supposed to stay in bed for several weeks. On one memorable occasion, the visiting midwife caught me hoovering and gave me a huge lecture about leaving a motherless child if I persisted with such stupid actions.

I had some help too, as Graham's mum was living with us at the time.

In fact, she had already been sharing the house with him for several years prior to our marriage. He wanted to stay in his house as it was near his work and his mum and dog were happy there, so I very reluctantly sold my Eastbourne house as we couldn't afford to maintain both. Then, I moved into his home.

It had been a great wrench for me as I loved my little house, but I wanted to please my new husband.

Moving in with your mother-in-law is not ideal, particularly when you are in your forties and an independent and successful career girl, but I was determined to make it work.

Fortunately, I had still been working full-time until I had Lucy, so I had appreciated having her there to do most of the housework and cook our meals during the week. It was a little intrusive, however, and made me realise why Mum had been so resentful at having to spend so much of her early married life living with her in-laws.

I was grateful that Audrey, my mother-in-law, was there whilst I was confined to bed for the first few weeks. She was happy too, as that meant she got the chance to cuddle baby Lucy as often as she liked. Having said that, Lucy was really only happy when she was snuggled up to me, breastfeeding at all times of the day or night. No strict regimens for us, which of course frustrated Audrey, as in her day, babies were treated quite differently.

Once I was allowed to get up and about, there was no stopping us. I had no money, having given up my well-paid job, but I had made some new friends at antenatal classes and we formed our own baby club. This was basically just an excuse for us new mums to meet up once a week, share our experiences, and give each other moral support. I was by far the eldest, but the other mums were all kind and treated me as their equal. We held these meetings in our own homes on a rota basis for several years, and because all our babies were born within a month of each other, we also arranged joint parties for their birthdays and at Christmas, in addition to the private birthday celebrations we held for friends and family. Lucy's first little friends came from this group. There was India, Jodie, Katie, Jasmine, Rebecca, Hannah, Louisa, William, Luke, and Thomas.

After a while, I hated having to ask Graham for money. I had been financially independent for so many years and rather resented being beholden to someone else.

But I adored being a mother, so it was a very small price to pay.

I had hoped to get Lucy christened in our ancient village church, but Graham was rather against the idea as he did not believe in God.

I still had my faith, the same simple faith I had learnt as a small child, but stupidly, I gave in to his wishes.

Already I was compromising too much, just to keep him happy.

When Lucy was still only tiny, Becky, one of the mums from our baby club, approached me. She wanted to go back to work three days a week and wondered if I would be willing to care for Katie. As Lucy and Katie got on well and we needed the money, I reluctantly agreed.

I was reluctant, as I had been thoroughly enjoying being a new mum and having my Lucy around all day, every day, to care for. I had given up my well-paid job with Cancer Research as I wanted to spend all my time with my baby. But I had to be sensible. Graham was a teacher so he earnt a reasonable salary, but we had a big mortgage and the extra money would certainly come in handy.

I contacted the local council, and after attending a first aid course, having police checks, home inspections, and making a few small alterations to the house with child safety gates and cupboard locks, I became a registered childminder.

Lucy and Katie were already good friends, so it was an easy transition for her to become part of our family. In time, as word got around the village and the council advertised my services, we were joined by baby Timothy, George, and Kitty. It was hard work and a little traumatic caring for other people's children, but we were a happy little bunch. It was very good for Lucy to have lots of small friends to play with and to learn to share her toys.

The first couple of years of Lucy's life passed very happily, but far too quickly.

Graham was a great help with the little ones when he was at home and he was a wonderful father to Lucy, taking her on long walks with the dog on the Red Road. I think they had rather too much fun, as we ended up having to buy new buggies every few months due to excessive use!

I could tell that Graham was getting a bit unsettled in his job. He loved teaching the kids, but wasn't so fond of all the school dramas and politics. He was doing a lot of casual building work at weekends and in the school holidays, but we were still struggling financially.

One day, Graham casually mentioned a scheme he was interested in: a year's long teaching exchange through the League of Commonwealth Teachers.

Apparently, you could apply to swap lives and homes with another teacher and then spend a year in Canada, Australia, or New Zealand.

I was thrilled; another adventure loomed.

Lucy was still only two years old, so it was the ideal time to go travelling.

He applied and was offered a placement in Auckland, New Zealand.

I was so excited.

Although I had visited Australia, I had never been to New Zealand; of course, it was right next door to my beloved Fiji.

ANOTHER ADVENTURE

We made our plans and found Graham's mum a flat near his brother to move into during our absence. I retired from my childminding duties and began to pack for our big adventure. I bade sad farewells to my family, especially my parents, my sisters Carol and Margaret, and my little nieces and nephews: Claire, Paul, Yvonne, Melanie, and Matthew.

We left England just after Christmas in 1996 and stopped en route for a few days in Bangkok, Hong Kong, and Sydney. It was a wonderful introduction to the world for our little Lucy and she handled it with great aplomb. The furthest afield she had been 'til that point was to stay in the French countryside with our friends Sam and small India. Therefore, it was a big adventure for all of us.

The hotel in Bangkok was fabulous - not expensive, but very luxurious. On our first night there, we ventured out to have dinner. The noise, traffic, and sheer number of people was pretty overwhelming, and we were tired after the long flight. Wanting to ensure that Lucy ate something, we reluctantly popped into a McDonald's where she was thrilled to receive a small, purple, plastic elephant with her Happy Meal. Coming out into the humid street afterwards, her little voice piped up, "Mum, look at that elephant," and I was amazed to see a fully grown elephant weaving through the busy traffic. We had the most wonderful few days there; we went to the Grand Palace, saw a dancing show, and marvelled at all the little market stalls lining the streets. We bought clothes and toys for Lucy, silk ties for

Graham, and a few fake designer watches for me! We never returned to McDonald's, but ate instead at the local supermarket, sitting at the counter watching the dishes being cooked. Not being able to speak Thai, we ordered by just pointing to whichever dish appeared to be the most delicious.

We were sad when the time came to leave Bangkok, but decided we would stop over there again at the end of the year, on our return journey.

Next we went to Hong Kong. The hotel room this time was much smaller but it didn't really matter, as we spent most of our time out and about sightseeing. We roamed the streets, visited the night markets, and went on the Star Ferry and up in the cable car to the Peak. We ate lots of delicious food and Lucy became an expert with chopsticks. We were honestly quite fortunate that she was such an easy little girl and would try most things. We caught the local bus 'round to Stanley Bay, and after dragging Lucy away from posing with all the coloured concrete statues, we bought a few things at the market.

One of these items was a rather striking white t- shirt for Graham, which featured a large pair of red chopsticks and the words, "The Great Chinese Takeaway."

It was 1997, the year when the colony of Hong Kong was due to be handed back to China. We had had several discussions with the locals about their fears relating to this change.

After leaving Hong Kong, we were headed for Sydney. I had pre-booked a hotel there for us in what sounded like a nice location. When we arrived in Kings Cross, we realised my error.

In 1997, the area was still a bit seedy, and as the hotel had no restaurant, we were forced to go out and find breakfast. These days that would always be my preference, but I wasn't such a seasoned traveller then, so we opted again for a safe McDonald's option. Lucy woke very early on the first morning, so at about 5.30am, she and Graham set off in search of a Sausage 'N Egg McMuffin.

"Oh Mum, it was so exciting," said my almost three-year-old little girl on their return.

"There were lots of bright lights and clubs and ladies in sparkly dresses, who all smiled at me and Dad."

Graham explained to me afterwards that the lights were from the strip clubs and the ladies in sparkly dresses were obviously ladies of the night, just finishing their shifts!

We had a wonderful time in Sydney. We visited all the tourist attractions of course, and Lucy hopped with the kangaroos at the zoo. Again, we vowed that we would come back one day and explore more of this lovely city.

Finally, we boarded a flight for New Zealand. There were some other exchange teachers and their families on board, so the journey passed quickly as we swapped tales of our travels and exchanged our phone numbers and addresses.

Landing in Auckland, we were met by a friend of our exchange family and driven to their house on the outskirts of Albany. Now just another busy suburb of Auckland, back then it seemed almost like the country, surrounded by bush.

It didn't take very long at all to get settled, and whilst Graham went off every day to his teaching job, Lucy and I explored our new home. We made some friends, joined music classes, and spent days at the playground and the beach.

Almost every weekend we would all get in the car and drive around the country. We explored around the Coromandel, East Cape, Gisborne, Napier, Hastings, Rotorua, Taupo, and Tauranga. We went on a steam train to the Ag Fieldays, stopping at Huntly for hot pies. We flew to the South Island and went on the Alpine Express train, marvelling at the majestic snow capped mountains. We drove the West Coast, from Greymouth to Queenstown, then across to Dunedin. We went to the Albatross Colony and saw the penguins and seals on the nearby beaches. I ate my first Whittaker's peanut slab at a little motel outside Dunedin, and it quickly became my favourite chocolate bar in the whole world.

Sadly, although it was only a three-hour flight away and I was desperate to visit, we never managed to make it to my beloved Fiji during that year.

We drove up to the North Island, staying in a little B&B outside Dargaville and visiting the wonderful Matakohe Museum, where I was fascinated to learn about the Kauri gum trade. We went to the Gannet Colony at Muriwai, drove the car on Bethells Beach, and marvelled at the size of Tane Mahuta.

At one point, we decided to go on an official tour to the top of the North Island. People had told us it was sometimes difficult by car, and we wanted to experience driving along Ninety Mile Beach and sliding down the giant sand dunes.

After just a few weeks, I was already passionately in love with New Zealand and wanted to stay forever. There was something about the country that touched my soul deeply.

On our previous trip up to the North Island, we had driven to Rawene to catch the ferry over to Hokianga Harbour. On the way, on a deserted stretch of road, we saw a broken-down car and a Maori man hitching a ride. He had full moko - traditional face tattooing - and looked pretty intimidating. We offered him a lift and he climbed straight in the back of the car, where Lucy was sitting in her car seat. I thought she would be absolutely terrified as she had never encountered anyone quite like him before, but she took it completely in her stride and within minutes, they were chatting away like old friends.

Therefore, a few weeks later on our bus trip up to Cape Reinga, she was not in the least bit fazed by the traditional welcome we received at the marae.

We were welcomed into the wharenui (meeting house) and I instantly felt at home. It was the strangest feeling, to be so utterly comfortable in an environment so different from everything I had grown up knowing.

After the ceremony, prayers, and speeches, an old Maori woman came up to me and spoke quietly.

"I was watching you," she said.

"I think you understand us."

Suddenly, it all made sense - the deep connection I felt to this country, the feeling that I was home and never wanted to leave. Even though I could feel it, I had no rational explanation or way to explain it out loud.

We continued our journey onto Cape Reinga, and the strange feeling stayed with me even when a seagull swooped down and stole Lucy's favourite toy, Little Bear. He had been lying on the picnic bench sunbathing in his red shorts, and the seagull had obviously mistaken him for a jam sandwich.

There was no way Lucy would allow this, so Graham had to climb bravely down the sheer cliffs to rescue the little chap from where the bird had abandoned him, precariously hanging from a flimsy branch.

Our year in New Zealand whizzed past far too quickly. We travelled and spent time with all our new friends. Our neighbours, Lorraine and Will, were very kind to Lucy. Will worked for Tip Top and brought home huge tubs of her favourite lime ice-cream, and Lorraine, a very talented artist, painted pictures of the Seven Dwarfs to decorate our house for her 3rd birthday party. At Lucy's request, the theme was Snow White, so our friend Chrissie made a beautiful cake and I started a family tradition by making jelly caterpillars and a Twiglet house. My dear friends from the Fiji days, Leonie and Lindsay, were there in their positions of honorary aunt and uncle, and their son Barry, whom Lucy adored, thrilled her by turning up to the party in his Air New Zealand uniform after he finished work.

Graham seemed to really enjoy his year. He made friends with some of his teaching colleagues and went on boating trips and other outings. They even went overnight to Little Barrier Island. As a scientist and botanist, this was a big highlight for him. We went to BBQs, had picnics on the beach in both winter and summer, and were very sad at the thought of leaving New Zealand, a place we had all come to love.

But all good things must come to an end, and we were committed to returning to England for at least a year.

154

We bade sad farewells to all our new friends.

Lucy had been attending the Christopher Robin Nursery School on Schnapper Rock Road for a few hours each week, and they presented her with a children's Bible as a parting gift.

At the airport I was terribly sad, but I knew that we would return someday so I tried to stay positive. We planned to sort out all our affairs in England and emigrate within the next two years, to spend the rest of our lives in this beautiful country.

BACK TO REALITY

But of course, life rarely goes according to plan.

We arrived back in England, moved back into our house in Sussex, and began again.

I found it incredibly hard to settle back into my old life this time around.

Don't get me wrong - I loved England. It was my homeland and the place of my birth forty-six years earlier. Additionally, my family and friends were all there. But I pined for New Zealand.

This was the second time I had lived abroad and both experiences had left indelible marks on my soul.

However, reality stepped in and I had to stop dreaming.

To help the family budget, I again registered as a childminder, and in no time we had a full house. It was a busy, happy time with lots of small children to keep me on my toes.

Lucy was enrolled at the little village playgroup, Tiggers, which was a happy, nurturing environment that prepared the children for their next big step: going to school.

Balcombe C of E Primary School was the perfect place for her to start her education. It was a tiny village school with just over 100 pupils, set in our village in the beautiful Sussex countryside. Because it was closely connected and just over the road from the old parish church, the children would troop over there often, therefore, they learnt about the Christian faith from a very young age. This was not done in a doctrinal, pushy kind of way, but rather as an add-on, a normal part of their daily lives.

At Lucy's first school nativity play when she was only the tender age of five, she was chosen to play the part of Mary. How I pitied poor Joseph, played by a sweet boy called Sam, as my Lucy was rather bossy.

Every time the music played, Sam would get up and dance around until she glared at him and grabbed hold of his tunic to force him to sit quietly. When it was time to pick up Baby Jesus from the manger, there was practically a fight as they both scrambled to grab the baby!

Her years at Balcombe School passed very happily, and she made lots of good friends. One in particular, Kemba, is her closest and dearest friend to this day. They met as four-year-olds and have weathered many storms together, so I am sure their friendship will last a lifetime.

After Lucy's first few days at school there was a PTA meeting, and I decided to go and offer my help if needed. At that point in my life I had never been part of a big committee. I had obviously organised plenty during my careers with Barnardos and Imperial Cancer Research, but in England I had never had the time to join a group as a volunteer. Consequently, I had no real idea of how desperately volunteers were needed, and was rather surprised when I came away from that first meeting having been elected as deputy chair of the Balcombe School PTA.

This began a very happy and rewarding period in my life. I was still getting used to being at home all day and not earning much money. Under other circumstances, I may well have found myself a part time job now that Lucy was at school full-time, but I was committed to child-minding my little ones. I cared for several small children on a regular basis: Henry and Esme, Andrew, Sam, George, Kitty, and Katie still came occasionally. We were a happy little team. Having the other children around took away some of the pain I felt at being parted from my beloved Lucy while she was at school during the daytime hours.

The PTA role enabled me to use some of my skills and experience as we organised various fundraising events and supported the little school in whatever ways we could. We held Christmas and summer fairs, which managed to raise good sums of money. There were also jumble sales in the village hall, where the donated goods would be piled sky high and the dealers would be queuing at the door hours before opening time, hoping to secure the best bargains. We organised race nights, treasure hunts, fashion shows, and wine- and cheese-tasting evenings. I made some good friends amongst the committee; we had a lot of fun and worked very hard to ensure we could help support the wonderful teachers who were giving our children such a good and well-rounded education.

During this time, Graham became very disillusioned with being a teacher and longed for a change. Before I met him, he had spent some years away from the world of education and had retrained in the construction industry. This meant he had lots of extra skills and was able to supplement our income by occasionally doing building work on the weekends. He did not, however, feel that he wanted to give up his academic life entirely, so when an opportunity arose to combine the two, we jumped at the chance. Thus, a new pathway was formed for us.

We both studied and gained qualifications as NVQ assessors and internal verifiers, and we set up an NVQ assessment centre for the construction industry. The UK government had realised that, since the virtual abolition of formal apprenticeships, there was now a surplus of construction workers who had been doing the job for many years but had no formal qualifications. These people were most unlikely to want to go to college or evening classes to be trained for a job they were already capable of and experienced at doing, so a new fast-track system was introduced where they could be assessed on the job while they were working. This would take several months, what with on-site visits, question papers, and practical observations, but at the end of it, they would gain a nationally-recognised qualification issued by City and Guilds.

Initially, there was a lot of objection and resentment from the men themselves; after all, they had been doing their jobs successfully for many years and they were only now being asked to prove their capabilities.

We ran the business from home and employed peripatetic assessors in the various skills - bricklaying, plastering, carpentry, drain laying, etc. - on a freelance basis, as we required them. Graham was able to assess many of the skills himself due to his construction background, whereas I only had my property-developing experience, which was certainly not sufficient to judge anyone else's ability. This did not deter me though, and in the first few years of our fledgling business I would often go onto building sites (by invitation, of course) and interview the men, putting their minds at rest by explaining the whole process to them. During the course of this, I met some really interesting people. It is a misnomer, in the UK, that construction workers are somehow lesser than people who work in an office.

I found most of the guys I met onsite to be intelligent and articulate - not necessarily academic - but certainly interesting and aware of how the world worked. Almost without exception, I also found them to be very well-mannered and gentlemanly, although there was one very notable exception.

I was on a site one day in East Sussex - not far from Hastings, but quite remote. There were about ten guys preparing the ground for drainage, as a new housing estate was going to be built there. I spent the morning interviewing them in turn, and at lunchtime, one of them drove into town to buy us all fish and chips. Whilst we waited in the little portacabin on site, the youngest labourer suddenly asked me what I would do if they decided to "do a gang bang," and rape me. I was momentarily shocked, then managed to laugh and said that I knew they were all far too gentlemanly to behave like that. But inside, I was quaking. Within seconds, two of the biggest, strongest men got up from their chairs and literally carried the boy outside. After a few minutes they were back, apologising profusely for the lad's behaviour. That day, I learnt a lot about men. Whilst they may tell dirty jokes and swear amongst themselves, just about all of those men considered me a lady and were appalled that someone on their team had acted in that way. The lad himself came to apologise to me later in the afternoon, and I think (and hope) he learnt a valuable lesson that day.

That same day, earlier in the morning, one of the biggest and toughest guys refused to join in the assessment planning. However, despite being a little rude, he seemed to take great interest in the trade-related questions I was asking the other men. Later on, I quietly took him to one side and explained that if he liked, I could read the questions aloud and record his answers for him. This was perfectly permitted by the Qualification Awarding Body and was perfect for someone like him, whom I had realised could not read or write. It was a shocking indictment on the education system, that so many young people left school after ten years of education and were still unable to do so. In my years of working in this industry, I came across this problem many times. This particular man, who looked incredibly scary but was actually a kind and gentle soul, begged me not to tell his mates. He had worked with them for many years and none of them knew; he pretended to read the paper at lunchtime.

He sailed through his assessments with ease, and after I sent his official certificate in the post, he phoned me at the office. Apparently, his wife was going to frame the certificate and put it pride of place on their lounge wall. That man, in common with many others, had left school at fifteen and been made to feel he was a failure. Now after twenty years on the job, he had a certificate to say he was successful and more than proficient at what he did.

Moments like those were very precious to me. It was so good to feel I was actually helping to improve someone's life and well-being.

Having always had a morbid fear of heights, it was not so much fun being on a cherry picker outside a six-storey building on a windy winter's morning while wearing an uncomfortable, unflattering hard hat and still trying desperately to look professional.

In the early days while we were getting our business established and when I wasn't childminding, I often used to drive around the countryside, visiting building companies to explain our services. Because it was a fledgling industry, there was a lot of distrust about the feasibility of the whole project. However, as time went by, we established a good reputation.

We quickly outgrew our first office in the little bedroom, so we moved to the front of the house and the much larger bedroom. Then, even that became too small, and we expanded to the converted attic at the top of the house.

As our business grew and we took on more staff, I gave up my childminding business and devoted myself to this new one full-time.

I am incredibly lucky that I have always been very happy with my lot - whatever my lot happens to be at that particular time!

We had made the decision to work from home and not take on expensive, flashy offices or buy company cars, and we were all employed on a freelance basis. This was such a blessing when the bad times came, and although they seemed to come quite often, we always managed to ride the storm because we had virtually no overheads. That is the one piece of advice I always give people now if I hear they are starting a business: keep your overheads low and you can survive almost anything that is thrown at you.

We worked very hard, as most self- employed people do. Very often I would still be up in the office at two or three in the morning, rushing to meet a deadline. At that time it was a very paper-oriented business, and after a while I developed a very sore wrist from all the handwriting I was obliged to do!

Once the first few years of trading were complete, during which time we made a very modest profit, the government decided to subsidise the construction qualification. This meant that the workers themselves, or their employers, did not have to pay the entire cost. Because of this, the floodgates were opened; we became very busy and much more profitable. It was hard work, but very satisfying and of course, made us much more financially stable.

This stability opened up some new avenues.

Lucy was growing up fast. Life seemed to be a constant whirl of birthday parties, dancing classes, horseback riding, and guitar and piano lessons. Having grown up in a poor family and therefore unable to do all these things as a child myself, I was determined that my daughter would have every possible opportunity.

I often felt a pang of regret, or perhaps even a little envy, when I attended her dance shows - particularly the ones where she wore a pink tutu and ballet slippers. This was another long-held ambition of mine, if you can remember!

Our home was always a busy place. In the early days, it was constantly full of small children. Then it became a work hub, and Lucy would come home from school to find a line of steel-toe capped work boots at the front door, where our assessors had removed them before going up to the attic office.

We rarely took time off from the business, so holidays were not really a feature of Lucy's early years, although we did manage to go to France every summer to stay with our friends Sam and India, who had relocated there.

Lucy also went to a few scout camps. There were not enough girls in our village at that time to support a Girl Guide pack, so the girls joined the Boy Scouts instead and enjoyed several very muddy camping trips!

The teachers at Balcombe Primary School provided an excellent, rounded learning experience and Lucy flourished there. She was a bright girl, and thoroughly enjoyed the social and academic atmosphere of such a small establishment.

I have so many wonderful memories of her childhood that I could fill an entire book with those alone.

Suffice to say, just a few standout moments will be enough, like the time of the Giant African Snail, a much-wanted pet that turned into something of a logistical nightmare, but proved to be a great hit at the school summer fair's Giant Snail Race. Then there was the gold panning game, when we collected hundreds of small pebbles from the beach and took them home to spray paint, turning our new concrete-tiled deck a mottled gold colour forever.

I cannot fail to mention the Red Road treasure hunts. This started as a one-off, a cute little idea for Lucy's fourth birthday, but due to popular demand, we were still doing it some six or seven years later. Basically, I would spend hours wrapping small gifts in silver foil - notepads, pens, bubbles, chocolate - the exact same number for each child and all individually labelled. Graham would then head off half an hour or so ahead of the rest of us, and distribute them all along the quiet country lane. We have many photos of lots of excited children, standing at the farm gate by the homemade sign that read, "LUCY'S RED ROAD TREASURE HUNT," waiting to rush in and claim their goodies. Sometimes we had a dozen or more little ones and a few parents, so you can imagine the chaos. At the end of the walk, the children would all fairly distribute the gifts to their rightful owners, although inevitably some would never be found. Occasionally they would turn up the following year, looking a little tatty but still in rather good condition, having been buried under piles of leaves.

When Lucy was three, I decided to see if I had a brain. I was very conscious that my academic achievements didn't match up to the three teachers I had lived with in my adult life, so I signed up for an Oxford Open Learning course to do an English A Level. This was a year-long course, but I was very determined and would sit up 'till three in the morning writing essays, translating Chaucer into modern English, and reading King Lear, Mill on the Floss, and Maya Angelou books. I sat for the exam just four months after the class began and managed to just scrape by with a pass. Having established that I did have a brain after all, I then pursued other passions and signed up for a creative writing course which I began and loved. Then I spent a weekend at the Quaker Centre in London, doing a TEFL course (Teaching English as a Foreign Language). I was very excited about the future and had great plans for several new career paths once Lucy was at school full-time. Sadly, none of these came to fruition, as we started the NVQ Assessment Centre shortly after and instead all my energies went into learning about the construction industry and making our business a success.

As Lucy grew, so did our business; I sincerely hope she never felt neglected. The plus side was that one or both of her parents were always at home. Graham was an excellent father, so I always felt that our roles were pretty interchangeable.

Being Lucy's mum, is, without doubt, the very best thing I ever did in my life. She has brought me such joy and happiness and continues to do so to this day.

Of course, our life wasn't all perfect. Human relationships are never easy and we had our fair share of problems, but we were a united little team of three.

As Lucy entered her teenage years, life became a bit more complicated. She now attended Warden Park, a secondary school in the nearby town. This involved her getting the school bus, so for me that was another wrench. She was no longer safely tucked away in the little village school just down the road; now she was out in the big wide world, away from my loving supervision.

But of course, she thrived.

We experienced many losses over these years. My beloved little niece Yvonne, a beautiful and intelligent little girl, died horribly and slowly from Batten Disease, a cruel genetic illness for which there is no cure. She was my sister Carol's only child.

My darling dad suffered a major stroke and lingered for six months, unable to talk, move, or eat normally, and it broke my heart to see him suffer so.

My mum never recovered from losing Dad and spent her remaining years in a nursing home, unable to look after herself and becoming more and more distant over time.

I had wanted to nurse her myself at home, but the hospital was adamant that this wasn't an option. Although I visited her regularly for the first few years, I will bear the guilt of feeling that I abandoned her for the rest of my days.

Even through extreme pain and sadness, life goes on.

Whilst we are in the midst of mourning our loved ones, it seems dreadful that the rest of the world just continues without them. We are so lost in our grief and the utter unfairness of it all.

Lucy and I often travelled. Graham did not seem to have quite the same burning desire to see the world as we did, so once the family budget was healthier, we took off from time to time.

We went twice to Alabama to visit our friend Michelle, and I marvelled at the Deep South, the cotton fields, the great accents, and the fine old houses.However, I found the underlying and barely-concealed racism hard to stomach.

We went to New York and loved it so much that I later took Lucy and three of her girlfriends there for a few days when they were fifteen. I dragged them to see all the sights: the Statue of Liberty, Ellis Island, the Brooklyn Bridge, and the Empire State Building, but understandably, as fifteen-year-olds they were more interested in the bright lights of Times Square and all the shopping. I hauled them through Chinatown, 'round Central Park and Harlem, and even to Fifth Avenue on Easter Sunday to marvel at all the Easter Bonnets.

I visited Venice for the first time when I was 50. I went with a few girlfriends and we arrived late at night. By the time we had reported a missing suitcase, the old airport right by the water's edge was almost deserted. The last vaporetto had departed, and we were stranded with no means of getting to the island. Fortunately, one of our group members, Manuela, was Italian, so she went to a phone box outside the terminal and hunted for the number of a taxi driver. After a while an elderly, rather grumpy gentleman with his pyjamas visible under his coat came and drove us to the main vaporetto station, where we managed to catch the very last water bus.

It was pitch black, save for the twinkling lights of the city in the distance, and we had absolutely no idea where we should disembark. The water bus crisscrossed the Grand Canal, collecting workers from the now-closed-for-the-night hotels and restaurants, and we began to get a little anxious. Every time we saw a church spire or splendid-looking palace, we decided that must be our destination. By this time it was almost one o'clock in the morning, and a cold March wind was blowing across the lagoon.

Finally we disembarked, the only passengers to do so near the Bridge of Sighs. We dragged our suitcases over bridges and up and down old stone steps. Suddenly, we turned a corner into St. Mark's Square. It was completely empty - just us five women and the moonlight - and it was a sight I shall never forget. It was at this moment that I fell completely under the spell of this majestic city. The feeling has never left me, despite visiting it at least another half dozen times over the following years.

When Lucy was 13, we felt financially secure enough to take a few weeks off from the business and go on a world trip. She was adamant that she wanted her friend Kemba to come with us, so, having secured the approval of the school and Kemba's parents, we set off in December, just before Christmas, for our big adventure.

We spent Christmas in Singapore. We marvelled at all the Christmas decorations and lights, had afternoon tea at Raffles, and visited the Botanic Gardens. We stayed in a lovely hotel and ate far too much delicious food at the buffet restaurant each night. We walked alongside the river and decided not to try the new bungee jump attraction. They had completely renovated the whole river area since my last visit, and I was disappointed to see that most of the old shop houses I had seen then, some 20 years earlier, had vanished. They had, however, retained a few, which had been smartened up for tourists to admire. We went to Sentosa Island and watched the incredible light show, and much to Graham's disgust, we girls spent hours shopping in Chinatown and Orchard Road. I took them all out to the Haw Par Villa, an incredibly unusual and rather bizarre place. Built by the family who own the Tiger Balm ointment brand, it is a place unlike any other - full of gaudy painted concrete statues of sumo wrestlers, ancient warriors, animals, and mythological creatures. The most unforgettable part of the park is the section dedicated to hell: the most graphic and distressing images of what happens if you lead a bad life. Apparently they have regular school trips there, to advise children of what will happen if they behave badly. Perhaps this is one reason why the crime rate in Singapore is so low.

After we left Singapore, we were on to Sydney, where we visited the zoo and the girls stroked the koalas and kangaroos. I insisted that we went on the open deck Hop On Hop Off bus to see all the sights: the Opera House, Darling Harbour, the Harbour Bridge, the Rocks, the Queen Victoria Building, and Kings Cross. Although we didn't stay there this time, Lucy and Kemba loved to hear the story of the time Lucy met the ladies of the night. And then of course we went to Bondi Beach, which the girls loved.

All too soon, our time in Sydney was over and we were off to our next adventure, New Zealand. I was so very happy to be going back to a place which my heart had never really left behind. It had been 10 years since our last visit and we saw a few changes, particularly around Auckland. For me though, the country had lost none of its charm.

It was also wonderful to catch up with old friends and visit old haunts. We travelled miles, from Rotorua to Queenstown, where we took a helicopter ride and marvelled at the spectacular views. We gold-panned, went on the Luge and jet boats, sailed the Waitemata, and ate too many pies. We had the most marvellous time, as I knew we would. This trip merely reinforced my theory that this was where we belonged.

It was hard saying goodbye again to all our friends, but this time I had no doubt that we would return...

...just as soon as we had managed to tie up a few loose ends back in England.

Our final stop was Fiji. For me, this was to be the highlight of our trip.

It had been twenty long years since I had seen any of my beloved Fijian family, and I was so desperate to hug them and look at their faces once again.

I had booked us into the First Landing Beach Resort at Vuda, as this was the closest hotel to where all my family lived. I knew the Vuda area of course, as I had often visited there during my time living in Fiji in the 1970s.

However, this hotel had not existed then, so I had no idea what to expect.

The last time I was in Fiji, in the early 1980s, I stayed at the Regent Hotel on Denarau Island. This had been a beautiful, stylish hotel - the only one in that area - with a lovely sandy beach. Sadly it is gone now, superseded by all the modern hotels that make up the island today.

At that time, I had no idea that the First Landing Beach Resort, chosen for its location and convenience, would become such a big, integral part of my story.

I was thrilled when we disembarked. It was a small and quite traditional resort, much more like the Fiji I remembered than all the glitzy hotels I had seen in the travel brochures. I saw the disappointment on the girls' faces as we approached the resort, passing the huge oil refinery that sat proud, but rather uninspiring, just 'round the corner. They were obviously thinking that this was hardly the exotic, tropical paradise I had promised them.

As we stepped from the taxi, I noticed a very handsome Fijian couple standing to one side of the entrance. I turned to smile and say something to my girls, when the lady suddenly cried out, "Marama, is it really you?"

I suddenly realised it was Nasau, Naomi's sister, and her son, Mesake. The last time I had seen him, he was just a boy; now he was a very fine-looking man with a huge, welcoming smile. I was so delighted to see them both, I just ran into Nasau's arms. We hugged for the longest time.

If you ever get to experience a true Fijian hug, you will be so lovingly surprised at the warmth and care you feel while enfolded in that embrace.

I was amazed to see my Fijian family. I had been worried before leaving New Zealand that I would not be able to track any of them down. This was way before Facebook or mobile phones, and all my attempts to find Naomi had fallen on stony ground. She no longer worked at the hospital, which is where I had previously sent letters; she had no home phone, and I knew she had moved from her little house in Tavakubu village to a newly-built concrete house just outside Lautoka, but I had no address. I had managed to contact International Telephone enquiries to try and get her number, but the first few people I called with the same name had no knowledge of her. I had been getting desperate when I dialed the last number I had been given for Naomi Likuseli. The voice that answered the phone sounded just like my Naomi, but apparently, she was now working at Manta Ray Island in the Yasawas. I was puzzled, as my Naomi would now be in her early sixties, surely too late to be embarking on a tourism career. However, it turned out to be her namesake, young Naomi, Nasau's daughter, who I had not seen for more than 20 years. I was so happy I had finally found them. She remembered me; we had the most wonderful chat and she promised to tell her mum and Aunty Naomi that I was coming to Fiji.

So, here I was at last. Back on Fijian soil and reunited with my lovely family.

It was a glorious, happy reunion, and we made plans to see the rest of the family as soon as possible.

It seemed that my Naomi was not at home in Lautoka but was staying on the Coral Coast, a few hour's drive away, with her son Jo and his wife, Kara. She was looking after their little girl, Arietta, while they worked. So, of course, after allowing Graham and the girls to have just one day's relaxation by the hotel pool, I hired a car and dragged them halfway 'round the island.

En route, I showed them some of my favourite spots: Nadi Town Centre, Natadola Beach, Sigatoka town, and the Fijian Hotel. These places had all seen so much change after so many years. While I rather lamented these changes, I am sure they were great for the country's tourism business.

We finally arrived at the Pearl Resort and I asked the receptionist if I might see Jo and Kara, who were now expecting me. The last time I had seen Jo was when I left my house in Fiji in 1978; he was just a shy, skinny young boy.On my previous visit in 1986, he had been away, working on the Blue Lagoon Cruises, showing tourists the incredible beauty of the Yasawa Islands.

"Marama," a loud voice suddenly boomed across the hotel lobby. Within seconds I was enfolded in a huge, warm embrace from this magnificent giant of a man. My little Jo, the quiet, young boy who had shared my home for two years was now a fine figure of a man, who had worked very hard and now held a senior position at this smart hotel. He introduced me to his Kara, a beautiful lady whom he obviously adored.

His rented house was quite near the hotel, so he came in the car with us to ensure we found our way. As we pulled up outside, I quickly got out of the car; I was in such a hurry to see my beloved Naomi.

Lucy remembers the moment well. It obviously made such an impact on her.

Apparently, I spotted Naomi as she came out the house and I just yelled and ran towards her. We stayed there, locked in each other's arms for a very long time, both in tears. I cannot explain the bond we shared. It was the most wonderful, glorious feeling; we could always be totally at ease with each other, despite our lives and backgrounds being so utterly different.

Eventually, we pulled ourselves apart and I introduced Graham, Lucy, and Kemba to one of my oldest, most treasured friends. I will be forever grateful that they were able to meet and spend time with her.

Very sadly, her beloved husband, Semesa, had died just a few months previously, suddenly and without warning. I knew what a great loss that must have been for her and could sense her extreme sadness.

We had the most wonderful visit. It was such a joy getting to know them all again and meeting Naomi's grandchildren for the first time. When the time came to leave, I was dreadfully sad to say goodbye again, but at least this time, with our family's new-found financial security, I knew I could return before too much time had passed.

The rest of our time in Fiji went by in a whirlwind. We spent lots of time with other extended family members, we visited the Yasawa

Islands, and Graham and the girls learnt about true Fijian culture. By the end of our trip, I think they were all a little bit in love with Fiji and its people too.

It was hard for us all to return to winter in England after all our adventures, but the girls went back to school, tanned, and with a new knowledge of the world.

Tragically, disaster struck just a few months after our return. Little Kemba lost her Mum, Andree, who was snatched away quickly and cruelly from cancer. She was a lovely lady, funny and kind, who adored her two children and had been a friend to so many.

Our business continued to be a success, so we were able to return to Fiji the following year and spend time with our Fijian family once again, restoring long-lost friendships and establishing links with the new generation. Lucy's love for the country grew, and I hoped that the seeds sown by Naomi and I would continue to flourish in our families long after we were dead and gone.

In February of 2009, I got my heart's desire.

I had never got over my dream of emigrating to New Zealand. Hard as I tried, I just couldn't shift the idea from my mind. Although we were settled and successful in England and Lucy was flourishing at school, I just felt there was something missing from our lives. I hated the English weather, often so grey and unpredictable even in the summer, and I had come to wish for bigger, bluer skies and not so many people.

Obviously, after our wonderful year living in New Zealand in 1997 and spending two subsequent holidays there, I was seeing it through rather rosy spectacles. In my heart, I truly felt it was the right place for us.

Our business was slowing down a little. The government had removed some of the funding, so it wasn't quite as lucrative as it had been. When we were offered the chance of a job and permanent residency in Auckland, it seemed to me like a dream come true. In hindsight, Graham may not have been quite as excited as I was about the idea, but at the time it didn't seem to be obvious. Once we had got tentative approval for our visas, I got on a plane and went house hunting.

Because we wanted Lucy to go to Rangitoto College, which had a good reputation, we needed to be in the correct school zone. I spent several weeks trudging around Auckland's North Shore looking for suitable properties. The New Zealand housing market is very different from the UK, and Graham had a long list of requirements. In the end, I managed to find (with his approval, via the internet) a huge, three-storey, quite modern house with views of the sea and Rangitoto Island -- and a full size snooker room!

It took a whole year before we got our final residency visas, and that year was a whirlwind. It is challenging to cut ties with your existing life and start again in a new country.

We sold our house in England to the first people who walked through the door and the shipping guys spent four days packing all our belongings.

The weekend before we left, we held a farewell party; adults spent their time at the front of the house and Lucy and her friends were in the family room and kitchen at the back. Everyone was very emotional, and many of her friends were upset that we were taking her away. Although the farewells were very hard, she was coming willingly. Lucy had definitely inherited my drive, ambition, and sense of adventure.

Saying goodbye is never easy, particularly when you have lived in a wonderful place for so long -- almost 59 years in my case.

But, I was excited at the thought of emigrating to a new country.

OUR NEW HOME

Lucy and I travelled alone to New Zealand.

Graham had stayed behind to oversee the final completion of the house sale and the transportation of our dog, Sprockett. Despite having been diagnosed with a severe heart problem, there was never any question of bringing him along. It cost almost as much to ship him to NZ as it had for all our household possessions, but he was Lucy's precious pet. Although we were aware that the journey could be fatal, we had promised we would not leave him behind.

When we arrived at our new home in Rothesay Bay, it was still summer.

Our house had many enormous windows and no curtains or blinds, so for the first few weeks it felt as though we were living in a goldfish bowl. We had no furniture, as it was all on the ship on the high seas, so I bought a couple of single beds and a garden table and chairs which we used as our dining suite.

We had lots of fun exploring our new surroundings. We bought a car - a second-hand silver Mitsubishi Airtrek - and whizzed all over the North Shore.

Sprockett survived his long flight and arrived next, and by the time Graham arrived a few weeks later, so had all our possessions from the UK. Finally, it began to feel like home.

It was a good job we had bought such a big house, as it was soon filled with teenagers. Gatherings, parties, and sleepovers. I just loved having the house full of young people; they taught me so much about my new country and I very quickly became fond of them all.

Having spent so many years being childless and desperate for babies, I now had a house full of tall, handsome, beautiful teenagers, who all behaved beautifully in my presence!

Life was good. We lived near the beach, so Graham was able to walk the dog there several times a day and he enjoyed chatting to the other dog walkers. He loved to swim in the sea too, so it was a pretty perfect environment.

We established a nice garden, enjoyed the enormous lemons from the existing tree, and I made hundreds of scented bags from the multitude of lavender plants scattered around the garden. I grew huge, red geraniums in pyramid shapes, inspired by some I had seen years before at the Floriade exhibition in Holland.

Lucy learnt to drive, which, as all parents will know, is one of the most stressful times in your teenager's (and your own) life. Suddenly they are independent, able to whizz around the countryside under their own steam, in a lump of metal.

The years passed so quickly. Lucy went to school graduation balls, then 18th birthday parties, always looking stunning. Like most young women, she was totally unaware of just how lovely she was. Her friends would come 'round on Friday and Saturday nights and spend hours in her bedroom, trying on clothes and gossiping. Sometimes they were kind enough to let me join in for a while; those are some of my most treasured moments. It was such fun hearing their stories and realising that they were exactly the same as I had been at their age, they just had more opportunities to do what they wanted to with their lives. The old expectation that all nice girls should be married by the time they were 21 was completely outdated. Now, young women could achieve so much more for themselves if they chose to do so.

Lucy had a very nice boyfriend during this time. His name was Matthew, and we became very fond of him and his family.

It is very tempting to write down all the doings and achievements of my Lucy, but I am doing my very best to suppress my maternal pride. Anyway, those things are her story, not mine.

Suffice to say that she worked hard in college and did her bachelor's degree at Auckland University. I was so incredibly proud of her. She also did lots of part-time work to supplement her income, so was able to support herself a little.

Because we had made a good profit in the business, we were able to buy a couple of rental houses in Auckland. They were both pretty tatty when we bought them, but with Graham's building skills and my interior design passion, we were able to turn them into lovely homes and were very fortunate to keep the same tenants for nearly five years.

We had also managed to buy a plot of land overlooking the sea at Langs Beach, just a 90-minute drive from Auckland. We had actually purchased this land several years before, on one of our trips to NZ. This was long before we knew if we could ever live in the country. It was a beautiful spot, and after a few years we had saved enough to build a house there. We designed it with the help of Adam, a local architect. It was a stunning, two-storey home with huge windows to capture the magnificent views. It had an enormous, open-plan lounge, a black kitchen and pantry, and sleek black leather sofas with a contrasting turquoise theme to match the sea views. I even went through all my books and used just the ones with blue covers to go on the bookshelves, then scoured charity shops for blue-coloured glass platters and ornaments. It was a wonderful project; we had fabulous builders and the end result was just perfect. All was exactly as I had imagined it, right down to the last blue tea towel. We went to that house as often as we could. It was just a three-minute stroll to the beach, and our neighbours, Heather and Gavin, along with their children, Thomas and Zara, became our good friends, as did Heather's sister Christine and her husband Wayne.

This home was a very happy place. We established a lovely garden and often entertained our friends and family. I would sit on my fabulous window seat just gazing out to sea and think about how incredibly lucky I was to live the life I did. Lucy and her friends would sometimes spend weekends or short holidays up there, and it became a real family treasure, an heirloom for the future.

OF course, life is not always smooth-sailing, and we lost many loved ones during this time.

I had already lost my dad, and Mum then passed away at the grand old age of 93. Suddenly I found myself an orphan, and realised that no one would ever love me as unconditionally as they had. It was a time of enormous sadness, but I was happy to be able to scatter a few of Dad's ashes and all of Mum's in our garden at Langs Beach. This meant I was able to go and have a chat with them both whenever I felt my grief begin to overtake me.

My baby sister, Margaret, also died during this time, very sadly taking her own life. She was followed a couple of years later by her son, Matthew. Suicide is such a dreadful thing. There are always so many unanswered questions, so much shared guilt. Could we have done better? Could we have stopped it from happening?

I was now in the very fortunate position of not having to work, apart from doing the administration for our UK company. Graham was often away, traveling back to England as he was still running our business, but didn't seem to want me to be very involved any longer.

I needed to do something to give back a little to my new community with my new-found free time.

I volunteered as a mentor for Project K, an annual programme designed for Year 10 students (aged 15) to help them build confidence and gain life skills. I was paired with Vivienne, a lovely, rather shy Malaysian Chinese girl. After a year of spending time together, we had learnt a lot about each other's cultures and had both acquired skills in rock climbing, abseiling, night golf, and cake-making. She even tried to perfect my use of chopsticks, with no great success due to my total inability. I was sad when the year ended and we had to part, but thanks to Facebook, we have managed to stay in touch and she has done very well. I was delighted, a few years later,to see a photo of her looking beautiful, confident, and happy, at her graduation from university.

My life encountered a bit of a hiccup in my 60th year.

Graham was spending more and more time back in England, and often seemed rather unsettled when he returned. He had now gone back to teaching part-time, but seemed noticeably happier running the UK business and doing the maintenance on our rental houses. I was rather stressed, as it seemed that however hard I tried, I could never do quite enough to make him happy. He confessed that he was in love with someone else, a lady he had known before he met me, whom he saw on his regular trips back to the UK.

I told him that if he felt that strongly about her, he should go and be with her. Apparently, he was unsure if that was what he really wanted.

I was shocked. Until now, I had truly thought we had a good life together, and the thought of our little family breaking up just broke my heart.

One particularly hot day whilst this was still unresolved, and after I had spent all day rushing around, I had an accident. I fell over in our kitchen on the tiled floor and passed out. Apparently, I had fallen backwards and Lucy said it was like a horror movie; she found me lying unconscious with a pool of blood around my head.

The St. John's ambulance crew came quickly and I was put into a neck brace and taken to hospital. On arrival in A&E, I was whisked into a side room and examined. Apart from addressing and treating the damage to the back of my head, they wanted to establish why I had collapsed in the first place.

They were a little concerned about my heart, which apparently seemed a bit erratic. I assured them that it was fine and that I had just been very stressed, but they decided to do further investigations the next morning.

The doctors also decided to do an ultrasound to make sure I had no internal damage. The one conducting the test announced that my tumble had obviously upset my gallstones. I was horrified; I had no idea I even had gallstones. Until that point, I thought that I was an incredibly healthy person, particularly for a woman of my age. The next morning, under anaesthetic, they put a camera behind my heart and found a slightly leaky heart valve.

In a matter of a day, I went from being a healthy 60-year-old to someone with a dicky heart and a gallbladder that needed urgent removal. On top of that, they wanted to check my brain next to be sure that was normal.

Fortunately, after several months of further tests and investigations, all was well. My brain was fine, although rather too overactive. My heart was deemed strong enough to have the general anaesthetic needed to remove the offending gallbladder and finally, after several months of drama, I was back in one piece.

It was summer. The weather was glorious and Lucy was thriving, and eventually Graham decided that he did want to stay with us after all.

Very few people knew of the drama between us, so it was easy to paper over the cracks.

Of course, the shock and sadness remained with me for a very long time, but I have been blessed with a forgiving -some may say, doormat - nature and I was determined to make the very best of our situation. After all, it wasn't the first hiccup we had in our marriage. Ten years previously, after we had been married for nine years, without any warning, he had announced it was all over and he wanted a divorce. After a few traumatic weeks, he had changed his mind that time, too.

Whatever life throws at you, never give up. Just learn to adapt and change. This was my new mantra.

Grateful to be alive, I felt the need to give something back, to get back to doing some good in my community. When I spotted a little ad in the local newspaper from the Salvation Army asking, "Could you spare an hour a week to visit an old person?" I thought I had found the answer.

I should have realised quite how desperate they were when Lisa, the lady in charge of volunteers, came to interview me at my home the very next day.

Lisa and I are great friends now, nearly ten years on, and we often laugh about that.

She phoned me a couple of days later and asked me to visit Bernard, an elderly gentleman who lived alone with only his cat for company. The first couple of visits were a bit stilted, but we soon broke down our barriers and both looked forward to our afternoons together. I would often take him out for little trips in my car; he much preferred it when we whizzed around town in the little red sports car rather than the boring Mitsubishi Airtrek. We would often drive to the beach and just sit in the car, looking out at the ocean and chatting while we sipped our takeaway coffees. Bernard was very fussy about the quality of his coffee, and I would often get told off for getting an inferior cup for our visits!

Lisa phoned me a few weeks later to ask if I could spare another afternoon, so I found myself visiting Joan, a lovely, very independent lady in her late 80s who also lived alone. She would always have a tray ready for my visit with homemade baking and pretty bone china tea cups. It was fascinating to sit and chat with her; she told me stories of her childhood and showed me photos of the Auckland she had known as a girl. I remember how cross she was one day when her doctor refused to let her drive anymore. She was into her 90s by then, and although she had a stairlift at home, she was most indignant at his suggestion that she was incapable of driving. It reinforced to me that losing your independence is the most awful thing, particularly when you have always been an active and independent person.

Thus, I now spent two afternoons each week visiting my new elderly friends, but when I received an email from Lisa just a few months later, I groaned inwardly. She began her message with the words, "Pat, I am so grateful for all you are doing, and please feel free to say no..." But of course, saying "no" has never been one of my skills.

Apparently she had a new client, a lady called Henrietta, with whom she felt I would get on extremely well. She assured me it would only be a short-term commitment, as this woman was 96 years old.

Rita (Henrietta) and I did indeed get on well. In fact, she became one of my most cherished friends, and I looked forward to our Wednesday lunches immensely. She was tiny in stature, but huge in personality. We would chat for hours. Like Joan, she read the newspapers every day and was interested in all that was going on in the world. She enjoyed watching cricket and rugby and loved to hear all about my life. She even made a carrot cake every week for Graham, standing in her little kitchen with the mixing bowl on her Zimmer frame. She had been a widow for almost 50 years, but her spirit, optimism, and love of life made her seem so youthful.

In the end, I spent nearly eight years having these three lovely people as my friends.

But of course, inevitably, I lost them all.

Joan died first, retaining her quiet dignity 'til the end.

Poor Bernard spent his last few years in a nursing home, struggling with Parkinson's disease and the loss of his home and independence. He hated it there, so it was almost a blessing when he passed away.

And my lovely Rita, my "short-term commitment," lived to the great age of 103, still fully in charge of all her faculties. I miss her terribly; my Wednesday afternoons now have a big hole where she used to be.

I have lost so many of the people I love. Loss is the most awful thing, something you never really get over. Instead, you just get used to not having people around anymore.

But as Helen Keller once said: "What we have once enjoyed and deeply loved we can never lose, for all that we love deeply becomes a part of us."

I had not touched a paintbrush for pleasure in 42 years.

Of course, I had done heaps of painting jobs, renovating houses and doing up old furniture, but since the time when Richard, my first husband, had not been entirely enthusiastic about my creations, I had stopped painting just for the fun of it.

When one of my new friends suggested I might like to join her painting class, I politely refused. She was fairly persistent, so in the end, I signed up for a swimming class on the same day just so I would have a legitimate excuse for not joining her. As you may recall, I hate swimming and am really rather frightened of the water, especially following a near-drowning incident in Fiji.

Anyway, the lessons did absolutely nothing to improve my fear of the water, as the instructor was quite fierce and had no time for my wimpish behaviour. Therefore, in the end, I reluctantly agreed to try the art class instead.

The moment I picked up my brush and dipped it into the bright red acrylic paint, I was hooked.

Since then I have been quite prolific, producing many paintings in my own unique, simple, straight-from-the-heart style. I have held a few exhibitions of my work and have even managed to give a few away and sell some others.

My love of gardening continued throughout this time, and of course in the New Zealand climate, things grow much faster. In no time at all, I had a garden full of my favourite flowers: sweet peas, blue bells, calendulas, stocks, and daisies. My red geraniums flourished all year round and I gradually learnt about the native plants and trees of my new home.

Life in Rothesay Bay continued happily. Lucy and her friends all celebrated their 21st birthdays, graduated from university, and set off into the big wide world. My nest was now empty and I was bereft.

Lucy had gone to London to do more studying, and I was lucky enough to be able to visit her. In fact, I had been back to the UK every year since we emigrated to see my mum while she was still alive and to catch up with old friends.

Of course I missed Lucy dreadfully while she was away, but she tried to come back every Christmas to enjoy the NZ summer. Luckily, this meant it was usually only six months or so in between our visits.

It was always agonising when it came time to say goodbye, but I was glad she was happy, adventurous, and making her own way in the world.

We travelled to Fiji often. It was so easy, just a three-hour flight from Auckland and I revelled in seeing all my beloved Fijian friends and family. There were always new babies to cuddle and small children who seemed to be growing up so quickly. Of course, there was sadness too. Naomi's younger sisters, Taina and SaluSalu had died, as had both Ratu Meli and Sarah, whose wedding I had attended in Lautoka all those years ago. We lost young Naomi to breast cancer and Mesake, her lovely brother, died suddenly, leaving two young children fatherless.

We always stayed at First Landings on our Fijian visits, and by now we had come to know many of the staff members very well. That little resort epitomises much of what is good about Fiji and its people.

One day, we noticed that First Landings was advertising land for sale. They were planning to extend the resort to include private villas, suitable for rental or private use. We wandered up to take a look and remarked how wonderful it would be to own one ourselves. Lucy and I then then took a taxi into Lautoka town to go to the market and buy some pineapples.

On our return, Graham was sitting on the bed, surrounded by bits of paper. He announced that he had been doing some calculations and thought that we should buy a plot, then save enough money to build a house there. I was quite overcome. This would be such a dream, to own a house in my beloved Fiji.

And so we did. It took several months to get approval for a sublease from the TLTB (Native Land Trust Board), but then we set about finding a suitable builder.

Building a house in the tropics is a risky business when you are not there to oversee it, so we were very happy to be introduced to a young Kiwi guy who had already built a couple of places at the resort. He took us to see his own home along with another he had built, and we were incredibly impressed with the standard of his work. Our NZ architect, Adam, had already drawn up the house plans, and this guy gave us a quote that we were happy to accept.

We then left it to the two of them to finalise things, and we sat back and waited. I, of course, had already planned the interior down to the last table lamp, and I began to sew cushion covers and purchase stylish plastic glasses to be used around the pool area.

Several months later I was sitting at Auckland Airport, waiting to catch a flight to Fiji, when my phone rang. I was only going for a few days to catch up with Naomi and Graham had decided to stay at home and look after Sprockett. The phone call was from Adam, our architect, who had just received another quote from the builder. It was almost double the original one we were given. Apparently, this builder had also already submitted our plans to Lautoka Council, obviously assuming that we would accept his inflated price. I was absolutely furious. By now, you may have thought me to be a simple, forgiving soul - a doormat, even - but I do have a tough side and on the odd occasions when I get really angry, apparently I am scary.

Fortunately, I am usually able to control my temper, but not this time. I remember sitting in the Koru lounge, alternating between anger and tears. This builder was incredibly arrogant, would not discuss or change his new quote at all, and did not understand why

I was making such a fuss. I spoke to Graham and we agreed to cut our losses and let this man go. If he could not be as good as his word, what else would he do once we were fully committed to a contract with him? In hindsight, it turned out to be a very wise decision, as he went on to cheat several other people in the same way. Some of them even ended up with unfinished houses and many lost huge amounts of money.

So, we were back to square one.

We owned a beautiful piece of land in a lovely spot, just one back from the beach. I spent weeks trawling the internet, seeking out suitable builders. Having lived in Fiji, I knew the pitfalls, so was wary of people who promised the earth but probably couldn't deliver it. By now, we had our plans approved, but no one to build them into reality. I was getting desperate.

A few months later in the hotel bar, we were talking to Jim, the hotel owner, about our problem. He mentioned a young Fijian Indian guy who had done a lot of work at the hotel. We met Viren that same afternoon and gave him our plans. Graham and I were leaving the following morning to return to Auckland, and he turned up just after breakfast with his quote. This quote was much more realistic than the other guys, and as we both liked him and felt confident in his abilities, we offered him the job then and there.

It was the best thing we could have done.

In less than a year, he had built us the most magnificent beach house, exactly to our specifications: a single-storey white building with an enormous open-plan lounge, kitchen, dining room, and four bedrooms, all with their own bathrooms. There was a swimming pool set in beautifully landscaped tropical gardens filled with frangipanis and hibiscus flowers. It was exactly what we had envisioned and I was so excited, imagining my future grandchildren frolicking in the beautiful pool with all the little Fijian children in our family whilst Naomi and I relaxed on the sun loungers, sipping cold drinks.

As Lucy had now left home and seemed unlikely to return for some time, Graham and I decided to downsize. I was quite keen to stay in the area, as I had made a life there and at this time was still visiting my elderly friends every week. We attended a few house auctions but the prices were very high, even for tiny, run-down cottages, and Graham suggested we look further afield. We had discussed moving to our house at Langs Beach full-time but decided against it, as although we enjoyed it as a holiday home, we felt we still wanted to be close to the city. We scoured the internet looking for suitable properties and found one that looked good in Puhoi, an old, Bohemian settlement and one of the oldest European villages in NZ. The agent advised us that it already had three offers and the sealed bids were closing a couple of days later, but said that if we were really serious we could look at it that afternoon.

We both fell in love with it instantly. It was just a few minutes' stroll from the village pub and general store, down a quiet country lane that reminded us of England. It was set in an acre of beautiful countryside, with only trees visible from all the windows, not a house in sight. And, we would inherit two sheep.

It took us no time to decide to put in an offer. I never had any great desire to live in the country, but this property was perfect. It was close enough to the village centre and neighbours not to feel isolated, but was also quiet and private, with a huge garden just waiting for me to play in it.

Our offer, which was more generous than the others, was accepted, so we then put our own house on the market. Unfortunately, our home took a while to sell due to it being a "plaster home." As new immigrants, we had never heard that expression. We had a builder's report done on it when we first purchased it, which confirmed that it was a very well-built structure that would likely never leak or have any major problems. However, at that time, the "Leaky House Syndrome" was a huge thing in New Zealand, and it seemed there was a stigma attached to such houses, regardless of whether they were sound or not. We had a worrying few months financially with a hugely expensive bridging loan, as we had to sign the Puhoi house contracts before we had sold our own.

We had a few silly offers, all for far less than the house was worth. In the end, out of sheer desperation, we sold it for a ridiculously low price to a Chinese gentleman who had never even set foot in it. We had done a lot of renovations; there was a new kitchen and bathrooms and I had made a beautiful garden, full of flowers, shrubs, and trees. I was very upset to learn from our neighbours that just a few days after completion of the sale, he had removed every single plant and tree from the garden, leaving it bare and desolate.

But, at least I had my beautiful new house and garden to play in.

On the first night we spent in the house, I stripped wallpaper from the hallway. Within a few days, the two of us had completely redecorated everything and I was beginning work on the garden, planning new borders. As I mentioned before, we had inherited two sheep, and I thought we should call them Doris and Audrey, after both our dearly departed mothers. Graham laughed and suggested that, as they were actually boys, they might prefer male names. So they became George and Ronald, named after our dads instead. Although Graham and I enjoyed having them around, Sprockett hated them with a passion. Fortunately, they were safely in the paddock next door; he often just stood by the fence and glared at them.

I very quickly came to love living in Puhoi.

The stunningly beautiful backdrop of majestic trees, the peace, calm, and quiet; the only sound was birdsong: tuis in the flowering cherry tree, pukekos strolling on the lawn. It was a taste of heaven indeed.

I joined the little village library, one of the oldest and smallest in New Zealand. I helped at the monthly village market, joined the hall committee, went to coffee groups and book clubs, and learnt to play Mahjong. I made some good friends and loved my new life. Graham was often away, back in England, but when he was home, we socialised with our neighbours and all seemed well.

He still wasn't interested in travelling, so, apart from our trips to Fiji, I would usually do my adventuring alone. When I went back to England every year to visit Lucy, I would often tag on a trip to France to visit Sam and India, or perhaps Venice, Spain, or Lille with Valerie, or Florence and Morocco with Lucy and Kemba.

One day, Lucy rang me. She was sitting in the library on a miserable, rainy day in London, studying Chinese art. Knowing and sharing my sense of adventure, she suggested that perhaps we should take a trip to China. So, just a few months later, she flew from London, I flew from Auckland, and we met in Beijing to have the most wonderful time. We visited the Forbidden City and the Summer Palace, and climbed the Great Wall. We explored markets and back streets. Lucy had done a lot of research, so we visited out-of-the-way art galleries in converted factories and old, derelict buildings. I marvelled at the giant artworks of KAWS, huge and imposing against the stark concrete and steel background of a deserted warehouse.

We caught the bullet train to Xi'an and saw the Terracotta Warriors, a sight so splendid it made me cry. We went to a silk factory and saw all the little silkworms performing their duties, and visited an old workshop to see beautiful lacquer cabinets being painted by hand. We were told they now sold primarily to middle-aged people; apparently the young people much prefer Ikea.

I had booked local, English-speaking guides for a couple of days in each place. Neither of us could speak Mandarin, so in this way we could be sure we were using our time wisely to see all the sights. In Xi'an, our guide introduced herself as Linda, and both her and our lady driver were so excited about our plans. "You are the first six-star guests I have ever had!" she exclaimed on meeting us at the train station. Both she and the lady driver, whose name we were never allowed to know, seemed extremely excited about our choice of hotel. Driving from the airport, Linda kept pointing out other hotels, saying that they were only five-star -- not as good as ours.

She was right. Our hotel was splendid. It was not aesthetically appealing, just a huge concrete construction built during the Cultural Revolution to house important party members and visiting dignitaries. Inside, however, it was unbelievably luxurious. There were huge, glittering chandeliers and shiny marble floors. Linda insisted on joining us as we checked in at the reception desk, sitting on a soft velvet couch, sipping jasmine tea, and being attended to by a beautiful young woman in a dinner suit. By the time we reached our room, I was pretty anxious. Had I misread the information on the website? Maybe I had missed a few noughts from the price. Surely all this luxury couldn't be had for the price we had paid?

But it was right. After scrutinising the prices in the room brochure, I could relax. In fact, we were so relaxed that I allowed Lucy to send a few items to the hotel laundry. They came back exquisitely pressed and presented in a beautiful box. Unfortunately, the cost of such service was almost the same as a decent dinner for two with wine, so we decided not to repeat the process!

The next morning, we rose early to have breakfast before Linda arrived to take us to see the Terracotta Army. We had arranged to meet Linda and our driver outside the hotel at 8am, so were surprised to see them both, an hour early, lounging in velvet chairs in the hotel lobby. Apparently, they just wanted to experience some of that luxury for themselves!

Our few days in Xi'an passed in a flurry.

Apart from all the sightseeing, Lucy and I visited shops and markets, buying rice paper paintings, embroidered cushions, silk pyjamas, and tea sets. I even bought a replica of a Terracotta Warrior from a small factory who promised to ship it back to NZ for me. We went on these shopping trips alone and enjoyed the experience, although we found the sight of row upon row of roasted baby ducks and fried seahorses rather distressing.

On our last morning, Linda and the lady driver arrived early to collect us. Our luggage had already been taken downstairs, so Lucy and I descended the elaborate staircase with just our hand luggage.

"But, where is all your shopping?" Linda exclaimed, as she momentarily stopped yelling instructions to our driver and another man as to the best way to load our suitcases.

When we told her that we had managed to squeeze it all into our three large suitcases, her face dropped.

"But you went shopping; where are all your bags? Your Gucci and Prada bags?"

Poor Linda. She was so disappointed when I told her that all our shopping had come from cheap but fascinating little shops, or even markets. She was crestfallen.

"But, you are my first ever six-star guests. I was telling all my friends about you."

She was very quiet on the way back to the train station. We had obviously really let her down.

We caught the bullet train to Shanghai and spent a couple of days exploring that fascinating city as well, before we bade our sad farewells to China. We both had a wonderful time and were determined to return one day.

Lucy went back to her life in London and I returned to Puhoi. I missed her terribly, but was determined to try and enjoy life, even though my nest now felt so empty.

I continued painting, and lusted after using one of the garden sheds as my studio. Unfortunately, Graham had already filled it with stuff - apparently, *highly* important gardening equipment and tools. We had two other sheds, both also filled to the brim with essential items, and despite my pleas, they remained out of bounds to me and my easels.

After returning to New Zealand, I booked myself into a weekend stone carving course and had the most wonderful time. At first I thought I had made the most dreadful mistake, as I had to use a handsaw to cut through a huge chunk of Oamaru stone. It was such hard work, obviously I had neither the technique nor the muscles for such a job. After an hour of trying to accomplish this, I was just about ready to give up. There were only three of us in the course and the other two, a carpenter and an ex-Olympic athlete -- both much younger than me -- seemed to be coping okay. Our lecturer obviously sensed I was flagging; I was so tired and frustrated that I was pretty close to tears when he sensibly suggested a tea break.

Encouraged by the others and fortified with coffee and Tim Tams, I returned to my table and the offending lump of stone.

"Okay," said my lovely teacher, a master stonemason and sculptor himself. "I think that's good enough, why don't you start working with the chisel now?" Within half an hour, I had made progress. My planned Easter Island head was starting to take shape and I was loving the whole process. In my imagination, I had now become a medieval stonemason, erecting some of the finest ancient cathedrals. That carving now sits proudly in my garden and is weathering beautifully.

By this point, I had begun to sense that Graham was a little unsettled again. He didn't really enjoy the relief teaching he was doing, and although we had enough money to maintain a good lifestyle, he constantly felt that it wasn't enough. He was still going back to England on a regular basis, and although I obviously worried about his loyalty, I tried very hard to ensure his happiness.

He then announced that he thought we should sell our two rental properties in Auckland and use some of the money to pay off debts. With the rest, he wanted to buy a couple of houses down south in a cheaper area. I was happy with the way things were; we had good tenants and a nice, regular income. But, despite my reservations, I agreed.

The Auckland houses both sold quickly. They were nice homes and our tenants had looked after them very well.

We began to search further afield and finally found a little old villa in Marton, in the Rangitikei region, just half an hour from Palmerston North, on the way to the capital, Wellington.

I flew there alone, met the agent, and fell in love with the little house, although it was in a pretty shabby state. It was for sale for an absolute fraction of the price of our Auckland properties, so I persuaded Graham it was worth our consideration.

Within a few weeks, it was ours. We decided to do most of the work ourselves, but obviously, we needed to employ an electrician to do the complete rewiring needed, as well as a plumber to replace all the old faulty pipes, toilets, and water heaters. For the most part though, it would be our little adventure.

We packed up my car with assorted tools, ladders, spades, and bedding, and off we set. Sprockett was a bit disgruntled during the long, seven-hour journey, as we only stopped a couple of times for coffee and loo breaks. Every time he tried to shift his position, he risked being squashed under a pile of duvets.

Graham wasn't willing to pay for us to stay in a motel while we worked on the house, so we spent several trips, three to four weeks each time, sleeping on airbeds on a cold floor in a rat infested house, with no hot water or flushing loo. However, we survived and actually had a lot of fun. It is incredibly satisfying turning an old, rather derelict house into something beautiful, and of course I could satisfy my interior design whims. I enjoyed my visits to the local Mitre 10 and Bunnings, even occasionally venturing as far afield as Palmy - as locals affectionately call "Palmerston North" - to get more building supplies. Spurred on by our success, we found another old villa to buy and renovate in Marton, and so spent many more months commuting between there and Auckland. Eventually, both houses were complete and because they were finished to a high standard: completely redecorated, new bathrooms and heating, with new cookers, carpets and curtains, we were able to find good tenants for them.

We still had a little money left over from the sale of our Auckland rentals, so we also bought a house in Feilding, a lovely little town nearby. It wasn't an old villa this time, so it didn't need quite as much work and we managed to camp out quite comfortably there. Eventually, that too was finished. We could throw our old clothes into the skip and pat ourselves on the back. Thanks to all our hard work, three families now had lovely, cosy homes to move into and we could finally return to our lives in Puhoi.

I was shocked when Graham said that he thought we should also sell our Langs Beach house. We had built and designed this just a few years before; I had assumed it would be a family heirloom, something to be passed down to Lucy and her children. He now felt that we should sell it and use some of the money to buy a house in England, so that we would have somewhere to stay when we visited and so that Lucy could use it as a holiday house for her and her friends. I had put my heart and soul into designing the Langs Beach house and my Mum and Dad's ashes were in the garden; I was heartbroken. However, Graham's argument was that Lucy would probably stay in London for some years, and with the speed and timing of his plan, it meant that within just a few weeks my beautiful beach house - together with all the contents - was sold, to be enjoyed by a new family.

He quickly found a house to buy in England, in a seaside town on the south coast, not far from Eastbourne, where we had been married. It was ideal, a solid 1930s semi- detached brick house. Fairly derelict but with great possibility, and of course, we knew we could easily make a silk purse from a sow's ear. Although I was heartbroken at losing my beloved Langs house, I was excited at the thought of another project, particularly one that would ensure I could spend more time with Lucy.

Graham left for another business trip to the UK, promising to return in good time for us to go to Fiji a few weeks later, to sign off on our almost-completed villa.

During his visit to the UK, he took Lucy to see the new house in Seaford and she phoned me. She was excited. Although it was a wreck, she had seen our previous handiwork and knew we could turn it into something beautiful, a place she would enjoy taking her friends for weekends and holidays. Spurred on by her enthusiasm, I mentally designed the house, planned window seats, and bought metres of fabric with which to make cushions and bed covers.

Graham had only been home for a couple of weeks when he announced that he thought we should extend the Puhoi house. This had been on his mind since we bought the place, a couple of years earlier. I had always been reluctant; I thought that the house was plenty big enough already, especially now that Lucy would probably never live with us again full-time.

But again, he persuaded me, with promises of a larger lounge, master bedroom, my own personal office, and maybe even an art studio. Eventually I relented, and we asked Adam, who had designed both the Langs Beach and Fiji house for his help. As usual, he came up with a fabulously clever design which increased the size of the house without spoiling its unique character. Plans were drawn up and submitted to the local council.

I was glad to be at home after so many months away doing the renovations on the new houses. I loved that idea that I could now re-establish myself, catch up with friends, and enjoy my lovely home and surroundings. My new garden was flourishing and luckily, the sheep had survived our absence.

Additionally, I had to prepare for our trip to the UK. In just a few weeks, our Lucy was graduating with her master's degree and we were going to London to celebrate with her. I was so excited; all her hard work was paying off at last.

The week before we flew to London, we popped over to Fiji to meet the builder and sign off on the house. As always, I was so excited to be going back and seeing my extended family.

We arrived in the late afternoon and I looked forward to my planned visit to see Naomi the following day. We met with the builder, who had done a fabulous job; the house looked stunning and the turquoise pool glistened in the tropical sunshine.

Late that evening, I got a phone call telling me that Naomi was in Lautoka Hospital. I arranged to go there at 11am the next day, as soon as visiting hours began.

Early that next morning, I got a call from Jo.

My beloved Naomi had passed away, and I would never see her beautiful face again.

Everyone who has loved deeply will know the depth of my sorrow. The two of us had been friends for 42 years. We were two women from totally different backgrounds who lived two totally different lives, but we shared a great bond. I was absolutely beside myself, heartbroken.

Her funeral will live forever in my heart.

The Fijian way of grieving is much healthier than ours. People do not try to keep a stiff upper lip, but instead they allow their grief and sorrow to show. Therefore, it seemed quite natural for me to prostrate myself across Naomi's coffin, weeping loudly and not caring what others might have thought.

Another chapter in my life was over, but our friendship will always be known and remembered. I was happy that at least there were now threads for the next generation to weave. My Lucy already held my Fijian family in her heart and I knew they felt the same about her.

And so, my beloved Naomi never even got to see my lovely new house.

However, her family all came to visit the day after her funeral and it was a happy time. The kids swam in the pool and we adults sat inside in the shade, sharing stories of our Naomi and her life. I was so sad for Jo, Ma and Ralulu, who had all loved their mum dearly and would miss her terribly.

At the same time, there was precious little time to grieve, for just a week later we had to set off for London.

This time, Graham and I travelled to the UK together, the only time we had done so since we emigrated. Usually one of us had to stay at home to look after Sprockett, as Graham refused to put him in kennels. That was not something we worried about anymore though, as we had lost Sprockett a few months earlier and his body was buried in the garden at our Langs Beach house.

The first few weeks in England passed by in a flash. We couldn't start work on the Seaford house as it still wasn't legally ours, so while Graham stayed with his brother, I stayed with my friend, Valerie, half an hour or so away. Ideally, I would have liked us to stay together, in a hotel or an Airbnb, but Graham assured me this would be fine as it was just for a couple of weeks, until the new house was officially ours and we could move in and begin our renovations.

So, I filled my time buying things for our new home.

Of course, I already knew exactly how it would look, I just had to find the right things at a sensible price. Because it was going to be a holiday home I didn't want to spend too much, so I scoured the shops and the internet for bargains. Valerie recommended a wonderful second-hand shop in Haywards Heath, and in just a few days I had bought tables and chairs, sideboards, bedside tables, sofas, and wardrobes. I even managed to get a couple of brand-new, good-quality beds that had come straight from a show-house. I supplemented these purchases with beautiful bed linens, cushions, rugs, ornaments, and books, all at bargain prices. This little house was going to look pretty spectacular on a tiny budget.

Graham surprised me by buying himself a grandfather clock, something he had seen and admired in an antique shop in nearby Alfriston. I was surprised, as he rarely took much of an interest in the interior of our homes, but I was pleased he was happy and readjusted my mental plan to accommodate the clock into my design.

Lucy's graduation day was an absolute joy. I was incredibly proud of my beautiful, clever daughter and we took many photos of her in her cap and gown. There were some with all of us and some with just her and Graham, both smiling and looking very happy.

How wonderful that I, who left school at just sixteen years old, now had a daughter with a master's degree.

To celebrate, Lucy and I took a little trip the following weekend, to the Cotswolds. We were going to visit some Fijian friends, Seru and Bulou, and their two little boys, who were stationed at a British army camp just outside Cirencester.

We stayed at the Kings Hotel in Cirencester, which was a very pleasant place. Before going for our visit, we settled down on the comfy sofa in our bedroom to watch the royal wedding of Prince Harry and Meghan Markle. We both cried, overcome with not just the beauty and splendour of the occasion, but with what it seemed to represent. A hope for better, more equal and accepting days to come. Judging by the crowds lining the streets of Windsor, we were not alone in hoping for that brighter future.

We had a wonderful weekend. Lucy drove me all around the beautiful Cotswold villages and we had a delicious Sunday roast lunch at the Soho Farmhouse. I left London the next day and re-turned to Sussex, to stay with Valerie once again.

By now, we finally had ownership of the Seaford house and I was itching to get down there and get started with my designing. We were only due to stay in the UK for another six weeks, so I wanted to get on with it. Graham was already spending time there, but apparently the status of the progress meant I could not yet start; the electrician and plumber had not yet completed their work, so he suggested I leave it for another week or so. I couldn't even just pop down there to do any inspections, as I wasn't allowed to drive. Before leaving New Zealand I had gone to SpecSavers for a routine eye test and they had discovered I had a hole in my retina that needed urgent attention, so the surgeon was booked for my return in July.

Instead, I contented myself with wandering into Valerie's con-servatory and looking at all my purchases. The room was overflow-ing - cushions, duvets, and table lamps everywhere, but at least I would only be imposing on Valerie and David's good nature and hospitality for a week or so more, then I could move myself and all these treasures to my new little home.

Eventually, I was allowed down to Seaford to start working my magic, so I donned my working clothes and got out my sandpaper and paint brush. After just five or six days, however, Graham decided I was in the way.

Apparently I spent too much time chatting to the electrician and plumber, stopping them from working. He said I could go back to finish my work once they were completely done. This was not how we had managed our projects in the past, when I had been the labourer, painter, gardener, and general dogsbody. I missed feeling like I was an essential part of the team.

And I missed him.

It was one thing being apart when we were on different continents, but here we were, only staying a few miles away from each other, and yet, apart from the weekend of Lucy's graduation, I had hardly seen him for the whole six weeks we had been in England..

Still, at least I had a nice weekend to look forward to. He had booked for us, Lucy, and Kemba to spend the weekend at a lovely old country house hotel in Hampshire, a place we had been to before and made happy memories.

I was so excited waiting for him to pick me up to go away for the weekend. Although we had been married for almost 26 years, I still looked forward to spending time with him. I was very surprised when he was almost two hours late; he was usually so punctual.

He was quiet on the journey down, barely responding to my usual chatter. He had often said that I "warbled too much," so I tried very hard to contain myself and concentrate on the scenery instead.

Lucy arrived on the train from London shortly afterwards and joined us at the hotel. It was wonderful to see my beloved girl and I probably hugged her much too tightly, as usual. The three of us went to Graham's favourite pub, the Hampshire Bowman, to have dinner with one of his old friends.

It was a pleasant, warm, and sunny evening, Midsummer Day, the 21st June.

We had plans.

Tomorrow would be special, a rare family day out, and then Kemba would arrive after work to join us for dinner. I went to sleep in happy anticipation, dreaming of spending precious time with my little family.

I awoke the next morning to find Graham making two cups of tea in our bedroom. This was not unusual; he had brought me a cup of tea in bed most days of our married life.

I sat up in bed, looked across at him, and spoke gently.

"Are you alright love? I'm a bit worried about you; you seem a bit quiet."

His response will stay with me forever.

"No. I'm not alright, actually. I don't love you anymore; I haven't done properly for years. I don't want to live in New Zealand anymore. And our marriage is over."

I was stunned. For me, this had come from nowhere with absolutely no warning.

Surely he wasn't serious? We had managed to come through this kind of crisis before, perhaps we could again?

I spoke through my tears.

"Is it her again? The same one as before?"

"No, she died four years ago."

Somehow I managed to get through the day, although Lucy kept asking me what was wrong. I really didn't want her to suffer and I hoped that perhaps Graham would change his mind.

Ironically, we had a lovely day. We visited a stately home, had a cream tea, and pottered around a museum and an old market town.

I struggled to keep my tears in check and at one point, I went alone into a little old stone church, allowing myself to weep freely.

Towards the end of the afternoon, Lucy demanded to know what was wrong. We all sat on the grass at the top of one of Graham's favourite places, Old Winchester Hill, and I gently told her that her dad didn't want to be married to me anymore. And that was pretty much that. The end of our 26-year marriage.

A marriage that I had such high hopes for, and had tried so hard to nurture.

To be abandoned, suddenly and without warning at the age of 67, is no easy thing.

Without the loving support of Lucy, Kemba, and my dear friend, Valerie, I would have struggled to get through the awful first few days.

They were all as shocked as I was, but somehow, we muddled along.

I was due to return to New Zealand in just ten days' time to have my eye operation, and there was much to do in the meantime.

The furniture I had bought for the new house, together with all the stuff in Valerie's conservatory, had to go somewhere before I left. Graham made it quite clear that I wasn't welcome down in Seaford. So, I had to think fast.

Finally, I came up with a plan and fulfilled another long-held ambition… to have a storage unit. Working through my grief, I got a taxi, visited the industrial unit at Ditchling Common, and signed up for a little concrete room with a bright green door. Then, I rang the furniture shop and arranged for their drivers - two big, strong Russian gentlemen - to collect all my stuff from Valerie's conservatory and deliver it, together with the furniture, to my new storage unit.

Having realised that however long I gave him, Graham was not going to change his mind about our marriage, I also visited a solicitor and began divorce proceedings.

He had said that he would not return to New Zealand with me, so there seemed little point in dragging it all out.

I was very worried about my Lucy.

She had always adored her father, so hopefully there was some way, in time, that they could salvage something of their relationship.

It was a very sad and lonely me who returned to Auckland alone, to mend my broken heart and learn to carve out a new life. Again.

It was pretty hard at first.

I had been so sure that we had overcome the traumas of the past. But of course, in hindsight, I realised that I was obviously never enough for him, that whatever I did would not be enough to make him want to stay.

So, I carried on.

Not calmly, but hopefully and with dignity.

I had my big eye operation and learned to survive living alone. I missed having Graham around; I had always thought of him as my best friend. But I still had the sheep, so they got plenty of attention and probably far more tasty treats than they should have eaten!

I rattled sadly around in our lovely big house, knowing that I would soon have to leave it. I looked at the beautiful garden I had created, and I wept.

The plans for the extension to the house had already been submitted to Auckland Council, so although I would not be there to enjoy it, I paid more money for them to be finalised. It was better to have some approved plans to offer prospective purchasers than to waste all the money we had already paid by just abandoning the whole idea.

Fortunately, I have been blessed with a fairly sunny nature and a deep faith in God. Without these two things, I doubt I would have survived.

I had suddenly found myself abandoned on the other side of the world without the husband or daughter I loved dearly. I had no one else in New Zealand, no other family to turn to, and it was tough. Heartbreakingly so. But I survived.

A couple of months later, Graham sent me a list of all the personal things he wanted sent to him in Sussex. By now he had moved into the house in Seaford, the house we had bought together intending for it to be our English base.

I sorted everything carefully, packing up his books, furniture, tools, and clothes, ignoring the advice of well-meaning friends who thought I was doing too much for him.

I emptied the three garden sheds of all his stuff and turned the biggest one into my art studio. I swept it out, set up my easel, and painted, that very day, a canvas entitled, "Abandonment," a wild swirl of reds and greens on a yellow background.

Once that was done, I put the Puhoi house on the market.

We had thrashed out a deal of sorts, which meant I had to sell the family home and the three rental houses and we would share the money equally. He would keep our business, his pensions, and the Seaford house, whilst I would retain Fiji.

I fought hard for this deal as the Fiji house was so important to me, but sadly, as the months and then more than a year ticked by with no financial resolution, I realised that it was impossible. I was creating a rod for my own back.

Whilst I might have the joy of owning such a beautiful property, I could not afford to maintain it on my own for the long-term. And so, I made the heartbreaking decision that it too would have to be sold.

We had enjoyed such lovely family Christmases until now, but Lucy and I decided that we could not bear to go through the motions anymore. Until the time when she had children of her own, the two of us would celebrate the special day in a more unique way.

She was planning to come back to NZ in December, to spend time with me and all her friends. When she rang and suggested we go to a vineyard for a couple of days, it seemed like a good plan.

"Oh by the way, Mum, it's about an hour and a half north of Melbourne."

To my well-travelled, cosmopolitan daughter, this was just a quick commute.

But I wasn't so convinced. It meant getting to the airport the day before Christmas Eve - one of the busiest days of the year - catching a three-hour flight over the Tasman, staying in Melbourne overnight, then renting a car and driving out to the Mitchelton vineyard on Christmas Eve. It all seemed like too much of a mission in my rather fragile emotional state.

But of course, I agreed. We booked our flights, hotels, and car hire, and that was that.

The trip turned out to be truly wonderful, just what we needed after the trauma of the last six months.

The vineyard was fabulous, the food delicious, and we even managed to cope with seeing all the happy family groups around us. We wandered up to the edge of the vines at sunset and saw families of wild kangaroos. It had been the right decision, much better than just staying at home and moping about what might have been.

Lucy went off to spend New Year's in Queenstown with her friends, while I stayed at home and thought about my new future. Then, the two of us popped over to Fiji and had a very happy few days in our beautiful villa. Kemba, along with another of Lucy's friends, Paloma, joined us too, so I introduced them to all our Fijian friends and family and the house and pool were filled to overflowing.

It was incredibly hard saying goodbye when my girls left to return to London, but at least I would see them again soon.

The Puhoi house had sold after being on the market for just a few weeks, and I was due to move out at the end of January.

It was a very sad time, as I had really loved living there and felt like part of the community.

But hopefully, I could find something smaller and cheaper nearby.

Sadly, there was nothing suitable available in the same village, so I began to look in Orewa, the small seaside town just ten minutes away. Living here meant I would still be close enough to continue enjoying a little of my old Puhoi life.

Obviously my budget was small, so most of the properties I liked were out of my price range. I considered an apartment, but they were all pretty pricey too.

And then I found it, my new nest.

A small but sturdy, single-storey house in a nice residential area, with beautiful views of the bush. It had a reasonably sized and com-pletely untouched garden. A blank canvas.

Within a couple weeks of moving in, I had painted every wall white and had bought new carpets, doorknobs, kitchen appliances, and blinds.

I had new lighting installed and bought new bathroom fittings. I painted the front door bright red, planned the garden to the last millimetre, and installed new fences and decks. My credit card could barely take the strain, but I was determined to have a home of which I could be proud.

It reminded me of the time I had left Richard, thirty five years ago, and moved into the Town Hall flat. I had been pretty penniless then too, but had still used my credit card for wallpaper, paint, and new duvet covers!

The past six months had been very traumatic for me, but I was over the worst.

The three rental properties all sold quickly, so I was able to give Graham the money he felt entitled to and begin to get on with my life.

I travelled to London, to visit Lucy. She was coping incredibly well with her sadness and sense of loss at our change of fortunes. I had written to both her and Graham to try and restore their relationship, and I was glad to hear that she had been in touch with him. Although if I am truly honest, I was a little upset and jealous, feeling that he didn't deserve it.

It was wonderful to catch up with everyone in England during that trip. It had been a very difficult year, but my divorce had now been granted and I had some decisions to make.

I knew that I didn't want to return to London to live, as some friends had suggested. New Zealand was my home now, and I hoped one day Lucy would return there permanently as well. My little house in Orewa already felt like home, and I had begun to establish a garden and make some friends.

There was, however, the question of the storage unit.

I had been paying rent on it for almost a year now, and it was stretching my budget almost to its breaking point. The girls were about to move into an unfurnished flat in London, so I suggested they choose anything they would like. They took the beds and the sofa and the rest I gave away to friends and the local charity shop. For the big items like the wardrobes and chests, I asked the furniture shop to collect them, not for any return of money, just to solve my problem. The same Russian delivery guys arrived at the unit to take them away.

"But this is so bad; they still have your name on the "Sold" label. We can't just take them away and give you nothing."

I had told them of my situation and in common with most people, they had compassion for my plight. I think things like that make people aware of how easily their lives could be upended too, without warning.

With the furniture gone, I was relieved. I stood in that empty concrete room, which somehow seemed to represent my loss, and I felt a sense of completion, a lightness.

In the end, I had a wonderful trip. Lucy took me to Copenhagen for a weekend and then I went with her and Kemba to Morocco, Marrakech, and then to my favourite seaside place, Essaouria, where we stayed at Villa Maroc, a delightful little hotel in the Medina. I bought beautiful scarves, linens, baskets, and fossils. We drank tea with our friend, Hichame, visited the lovely ladies at the argan oil cooperative, and I bought silver jewellery from a charming Bedouin gentleman.

In Sussex, I stayed with Valerie and David again, but this time there were no enormous piles of shopping to litter up their conservatory. Instead we had fun - we went to the movies, out for lunch, shopped, and visited friends.

My friend Sam came over from France, and we visited the Poppy Factory just outside Richmond in Surrey. It was very moving and a place I believe everyone should visit, especially the younger generations who have never experienced war.

I caught up with all my old friends, ate, drank, laughed, and began to feel more like my old self again.

Jen and I went to the Mary Quant exhibition at the V&A museum and we marched around the exhibits, getting very excited to see replicas of all the clothes we had worn back in the 1960s. With Valerie and Sue I went to Lewes, and sat in the sunshine on the pavement outside Bills, an old converted greengrocers shop, eating delicious fish finger sandwiches. Then, we went to an old railway depot, which had been converted to a cinema, to watch *Rocketman*, the movie about Elton John's life.

It felt strange to be in the same country as my soon-to-be ex-husband, yet have nothing to do with him. The man I had loved and tried to make happy for twenty-six years.

So, early one sunny morning I went down to Seaford to visit him, unannounced.

Perhaps it was a mistake, but it gave me a closure of sorts.

The sad realisation that I meant absolutely nothing to him.

My last week in England whizzed past.

I helped the girls move into their new flat, had a long lunch with my old friend, Robert, went to a Lee Krasner exhibition at the Barbican, shopped for flowers in Columbia Road Market, and ate a delicious Sunday roast with my lovely daughter.

It was hard saying goodbye, but I would see her again when she came to New Zealand for Christmas and we would spend our last holiday together in our beloved Fiji house. I had already planned another trip to go to London, in May of 2020.

As promised, Lucy came home for Christmas and we flew to Fiji.

It was a bittersweet time. I had already agreed to sell the house at a much reduced price. It was breaking my heart, but I had no alternative.

It was expensive to keep and I just couldn't afford it.

So, during our holiday, we filled the house to overflowing and crowded the pool full of excited children. We went to the market and bought dozens of pineapples and huge watermelons, and we entertained all our Fijian family and friends.

It was a glorious time, but there was a sadness too, because we all knew it was the last time.

As Lucy and I locked the door behind us on the last morning, it really felt like the end of an era.

I sold the house with all the furniture, the table lamps, the cushions, and the bedcovers I had so lovingly made. I left the blue seashell china I had bought in France so many years ago, and the beautifully-framed tapa cloths and hand-woven mats. It was like leaving a huge part of me behind, but I had no choice. It was over and I had to move on.

I had often said that I felt uncomfortable owning so many houses when others had so little. Well, now I had my wish; all the houses and the shiny red sports car were gone.

After Christmas, Lucy went back to London. I was alone again.

This time, I tried my best to keep busy. I read numerous books and worked in my garden. I was still helping at the Puhoi Market and served on the Puhoi Hall committee. I played mahjong every week, did pilates, and met friends for lunch or coffee. I socialised with my lovely new neighbours.

My divorce was finalised at last and I had my decree absolute. It really felt as though my life was getting back on track.

Then, on the day of my 69th birthday, we went into lockdown in New Zealand.

Enforced self-isolation due to the COVID-19 virus. So, I made myself a chocolate brownie, put a candle in it, and celebrated alone in my beautiful, sunny garden.

I was sad that I couldn't go on my trip to London as planned.

I had so many exciting things booked: a trip to Russia, Helsinki, Tallinn, and Riga, then to Morocco, France, Spain, and Sussex. I had been so looking forward to catching up with Lucy and all my friends.

Like most people, I found lockdown difficult initially, and spent the first couple of weeks lying on the sofa, eating chocolate, and watching Netflix, feeling rather sorry for myself. Then, I pulled myself together and decided to write a book.

I spread myself across every space in the house, sheets of paper everywhere with wild scribblings all over them. I sat up night after night, frantically typing my thoughts into reality.

Writing has been the most wonderful experience. I have discovered a new career in my 69th year, one that has brought me such joy. By the time you read this I will have published two books: this one and the other, the first novel I wrote, entitled *Daisy*.

Life can be tough, but try to keep smiling through your tears. When you get knocked down, get up and carry on. You never know what's around the next corner.

THE END

AUTHOR BIOGRAPHY

Pat Backley is an English woman, who at the age of 59, decided to become a Kiwi. Now she lives in New Zealand, and when not writing, Pat loves to travel the world. She particularly enjoys spending lots of time in Fiji with her beloved extended Fijian family. In the past five years, Pat had also loved making trips back to London to visit her daughter, Lucy, who has recently and happily settled back in New Zealand - just down the road from her in Auckland! She also gardens, paints, reads, and loves activities like interior design, walks on the beach, and socialising.

In short she lives an ideal existence, which hasn't always been so easy, as these memoirs will explain!

1957 -Author as a schoolgirl
2019- Author with Jo (Naomi's son)